"You open a door when you open this book — a door that swings wide to unlimited horizons of knowledge and will enlarge the dimensions of your life."

SOUTHERN SPICE A LA MICROWAVE

by
Margie Brignac

"A Gourmet's Cookbook of French, Acadian and Creole Recipes"

PELICAN PUBLISHING COMPANY
GRETNA 1989

First published, September 1980
Pelican Edition
  First printing, November 1981
  Second printing, February 1982
  Third printing, September 1983
  Fourth printing, November 1984
  Fifth printing, December 1986
  Sixth printing, June 1989

.

Library of Congress Cataloging in Publication Data

Brignac, Margie.
    Southern spice a la microwave.

    Includes index.
    1. Cookery, American-Southern States.
2. Microwave cookery.   I. Title
TX715.B8463   1981   641.5'882   81-19241
ISBN 0-88289-318-1   AACR2

Manufactured in the United States of America
Published by Pelican Publishing Company, Inc.
1101 Monroe Street, Gretna, Louisiana 70053

DEDICATION

This book is dedicated to my children who always have faith in me and what I do, and to my mother who respects my dreams and expectations without question and makes me feel loved not for what I may accomplish, but for what I am.

"Every man should eat and drink well, and enjoy the good of his labor—it is the gift of God."   Ecclesiastes 3:13

Cover photograph: Phil Gould
Illustrations: Tim Louque
Graphics: Randy Norwood
Typist: Lisa Duhe
Proofreaders: Angela Harrell and Judy Lucia

TABLE OF CONTENTS

Appetizers ....Pages 1 - 11
Soups, Gumbos ....Pages 12 - 21
Meat and Meat Dishes ....Pages 22 - 49
Poultry...................................Pages 50 - 67
Seafood.................................Pages 68 - 93
Vegetables .... Pages 94 - 132
Rice, Jambalaya, Pasta,
    Grits, Roux...................... Pages 134 - 142
Eggs, Sauces, Corn Bread .... Pages 144 - 155
Salads .... Pages 156 - 164
Desserts .... Pages 166 - 214

FOREWORD

Welcome to the world of convenience — the world of microwave magic — making it possible for you to lead an active lifestyle and still prepare those savory meals your family enjoys so much.

With the time-saving convenience of the microwave, you'll soon wonder how you ever survived without this valuable appliance.

In SOUTHERN SPICE, I have combined the speed of microwave cooking with the heritage of Creole cooking to bring you some of the most delicious recipes in the Deep South.

Creole cooking is not the gift of one country or one race. It is the best culinary arts of Europe and Spanish America influenced by Negro and Indian culinary arts intermingled with a dash of the Deep Delta. SOUTHERN SPICE takes the old world flavor of new world recipes which have been handed down from generation to generation and presents them to you in energy saving microwave recipes you'll want to enjoy again and again.

So join me in the kitchen as we combine modern technology with age old secrets to toss together a souffle, gravy, or a fantastic casserole that tastes and looks as though it took hours to prepare.

I have truly enjoyed preparing and testing these recipes for the preparation of this book and I sincerely hope that SOUTHERN SPICE will make microwave cooking more enjoyable for you and inspire you to experiment with some of the most delectable recipes ever.

The recipes in this book were tested and timed in a name brand oven. This oven had a 650 wattage magnetron tube. The following hints and chart may help you in reference to your own oven.

1. If your oven wattage is:
Less than 650: add a minute or so to cooking time.

2. If you oven wattage is:
More than 650: subtract a minute or so from cooking time

In the front pages of the reader's manual for your oven there should be a chart or power setting guide with a name for each power setting. For example:

High	=	**100% Power**
(Named For Your Oven)	=	**90% Power**
(Named For Your Oven)	=	**70% Power**
(Named For Your Oven)	=	**50% Power**
(And So On)		

Use this chart to help you when cooking with other cook books rather than the one which came with your oven. If your book does not have such a chart, contact your oven dealer and obtain this information from him. If you cannot obtain this information from him, you may write to the folowing address and ask them for it:

Microwave Cooking Library
Dept. P3
5700 Green Circle Drive
Minnetonka, Minnesota 55343

HELPFUL HINTS

ORDER OF COOKING FOODS:

Foods that need to be cooked the longest should be cooked first. Foods which are considered dense because they consist of tightly packed molecules, such as **Roasts** or **Large Cuts of Meat** or **Poultry,** take longer to cook; therefore, should be cooked first. Foods which take less cooking time because they are more porous, such as **Bread, Cakes** or **Eggs,** should be cooked last.

WHAT CONTAINERS CAN BE USED:

Glass   **Ceramics**
Pyroceramics   **Pottery**
Straw or Wood   **Pyrex**
Paper (not brown or recycled)   **Corning** (not Centura)
Corelle (not the closed handle cups)
Plastics (only for warming or short time cooking with no fat or oil)
Tupperware (only for warming)

CONTAINERS NOT TO BE USED:

Metal   **Centura**
Foil   **Melamine**
Dishes with Metal Trim (Gold or Silver)
Tupperware (for long cooking or with oil)

DISH TEST:

Place the dish in question in the oven. Place a cup of water in the oven. Micro on **High 1 Minute.** If dish is hot, it cannot be used; if it is cool, it can be used.

SIZE AND SHAPE OF CONTAINERS:

Size and shape of the containers used in this recipe book may be slightly substituted. Keep in mind that **The Larger The Container, The Longer The Cooking Time.** A round or oval container cooks more evenly than a square or rectangular one.

STARTING TEMPERATURE OF FOOD:

The starting temperature of the food effects the cooking time. **The Colder The Food, The Longer It Takes To Cook, Heat, Or Defrost.** Therefore, foods taken from the refrigerator will take longer to cook or heat than food started from room temperature. The recipes in cook books are based on normal storage temperature. For example: milk and butter are usually refrigerated; therefore, when milk or butter is called for in a recipe, it is assumed it will be taken from the refrigerator. If onion is called for, it is assumed it is room temperature; therefore, if frozen onion is used, the time of saute'ing may be a little longer.

FOOD QUANTITIES EFFECT COOKING TIME:

The volume or amount of food being cooked determines the cooking time. **The Greater The Amount Of Food Put In The Oven, The Longer The Cooking Time.**

COVERING EFFECTS RESULTS AND COOKING TIME:

Covering creates intense heat and steam; therefore, **Covering Reduces Cooking Time.** Covering also reduces drying out of foods. Any food that you want kept moist should be covered.

Covers That Can Be Used Are:

Plastic Wrap: to cook faster and keep moist.
Glass Casserole Lids: to cook faster and keep moist.
Paper Towels: to prevent splatter and trap some moisture.

SUMMARY OF WHAT EFFECTS COOKING TIME:

Size Of Container
Temperature Of Food
Quantity Of Food
Covering Of Food
Density Of Food

ARRANGEMENT OF FOOD:

Because microwaves cook the outer sections of food first, the **Center Takes Longer To Cook.** When arranging food (such as chicken) on a plate or cooking dish, **Place The Larger, Thicker Portions To The Outside Of The Dish.**

When preparing small items, such as potatoes, muffins, cookies, etc., place them in a ring or circle rather than in a line. Do not stack foods. **Round Dishes Work Better Than Square Ones Do.** (A square edge cooks faster than rest of dish.)

STIRRING:

Because the outer edge of food cooks faster than the center, **It Is Important To Stir Certain Foods During Cooking** in order to bring under-cooked food to outer edges. Soups, stews, gravies and ground beef should be stirred often.

STANDING TIME:

Because food continues to cook after being removed from the oven, **A Standing Time Is Needed** before serving. This allows heat to conduct towards the center of the food. The denser the food, the longer standing time is required.

SAUTE ING:

The right amount of time in saute'ing vegetables plays an important part in the outcome or success of your dish. The time varies according to:

1. **Your Oven Wattage.**
   If your oven has a very high wattage (over 675) you may saute' a little less time.
2. **The Amount Of Vegetables Being Saute'ed.**
   If you are using a large amount of vegetables, you will saute' longer than a smaller amount.
3. **Whether Or Not The Vegetables Are Fresh Or Frozen.**
   If your vegetables are fresh, they will saute' in less time than if they are frozen. Also, vegetables which have been put in a food processor may take slightly longer because of the juices they have secreted.

UTENSILS

PICTURES	UTENSILS	USED FOR
1.	Glass Measuring Cup 2-cup 3-cup 8-cup	measuring Roux heating liquids making stews making sauces making candy saute' onions, etc.
2.	Round Glass Casseroles 1 quart 1-1/2 quart 2 quart 2-1/2 quart 3 quart	sauces stews rice vegetables small casseroles dips fruit custard
3.	Corning Ware Casseroles 1-1/2 quart 2 quart 3 quart 4 quart 5 quart	potatoes sauces vegetables small casseroles meat poultry (4 qt.) gumbo (5 qt.) soup (4 or 5 qt.) boil spaghetti
4.	Oblong Casserole 7" x 11" 6" 8"	meatloaf casseroles meat poultry cakes fudge fish seafood

UTENSILS
(Continued)

PICTURES	UTENSILS	USED FOR
5. 	10" Corning Browning Skillet or Casserole Dish	browning chops hamburgers eggs casseroles liver and other meats fish
6. 	Square Pyrex Dish 8" x 8"	Snacking Cakes dessert fruit buttered vegetables fudge small casseroles
7. 	Glass Pyrex Pie Plate 8" 9"	pies flat foods omelets quiche fruit
8. 	Deep Round Pyrex Dish 3 quart 4 quart	gumbo (4 qt.) rice (3 qt.) soup (4 qt.)
9. 	Glass Round Cake Dish	cakes stuffed peppers stuffed tomatoes bread pudding
10. 	Microwave Plastic Cake Dish	cakes bread pudding desserts quiche potatoes, any style

Appetizers

APPETIZERS

Artichoke Balls 3

Bacon and Water Chestnut Appetizer 3

Baked Beef Dip 4

The Big Dipper 4

Cheese Rarebit 5

Dipsy Devil Dip 5

Hot Cheese Crackers 6

Marinated Party Vegetables 6

Marinated Vegetables 7

Raw Vegetable Dip... 8

Crab Dip 9

Shrimp or Crab Dip I...................................... 10

Shrimp or Crab Dip II 10

Crawfish Dip 11

*"You can because you think
you can."*

ARTICHOKE BALLS

Utensils: 3 quart dish
Time: 5 minutes
Servings: 12-15

1 jar (8 oz.) marinated
   artichoke hearts
1 can (6 oz.) mushroom pieces,
   drained
3 pods garlic or 1 teaspoon
   garlic powder

1. In blender or food processor, put artichoke hearts and liquid, mushrooms drained, and garlic. Puree. Set aside.

1 cup Parmesan cheese, grated
1 cup Romano cheese, grated
1 cup Italian bread crumbs
2 eggs, beaten
salt and pepper to taste

2. Add cheeses, bread crumbs, eggs, salt and pepper. Mix well and roll into small balls. Roll in bread crumbs. Place in casserole dish. Micro on **70% Power 5 Minutes,** until hot.

BACON AND WATER CHESTNUT APPETIZER

Utensils: Small bowl
             Paper plate and paper towels
Time: 1 minute per slice
Servings: Approximately 10-12

1 can (5 oz.) water chestnuts,
   drained
1/3 cup soy sauce
1/2 cup cooking wine

1. Soak chestnuts in wine and soy sauce mixture overnight.

bacon slices, cut in thirds

2. Wrap 1/3 bacon slice around each chestnut and secure with toothpicks. Place about 12 chestnuts on a paper plate lined with a paper towel. Micro on **High** for about **5-6 Minutes,** or until bacon is crisp.

3

BAKED BEEF DIP

Utensils: 2-3 quart Corning dish
Time: 8 minutes
Servings: 15

2 packages (8 oz.) cream
    cheese, softened
1/4 cup milk
2 packages (2-1/2 oz. each)
    dried beef, minced
1/4 teaspoon garlic powder
1 teaspoon salt
1 carton (8 oz.) sour cream
4 teaspoons minced onion

1. In 2-3 quart dish, mix all ingredients. Micro on **High 8 Minutes.** Serve with crackers or chips.

THE BIG DIPPER
(Beef Dip)

Utensils: 2-3 quart dish
Time: 24 minutes
Servings: 12-15

2 tablespoons butter or oleo
1 pound ground beef

1. In 2 or 3 quart dish, put butter and ground beef. Micro on **High 10 Minutes,** mashing with a potato masher to prevent lumping. Drain beef.

1/4 teaspoon garlic powder
1/4 teaspoon oregano
1/4 teaspoon basil
1/4 teaspoon fennel (optional)
1/4 teaspoon rosemary
    (optional)
1 envelope dry onion soup mix
1 can (6 oz.) tomato paste
1/2 cup cooking wine

2. Add garlic, oregano, basil, fennel, rosemary, soup mix, tomato paste and wine. Micro on **70% Power** for **10 Minutes.**

1 cup sharp Cheddar cheese,
    grated
1 (8 oz.) package cream cheese

3. Add the two cheeses. Micro on **High 4 Minutes.** Serve warm as a dip for chips or crackers.

CHEESE RAREBIT

Utensils: 2 quart dish
Time: 8 minutes
Servings: 10-12

1 cup milk
2 cups American cheese,
 grated
1 tablespoon oleo
1/2 teaspoon salt
— dash of black pepper
1/2 teaspoon mustard
1/2 teaspoon Worcestershire
 sauce

1. In 2 quart dish, put milk, cheese, oleo, salt, pepper, mustard and Worcestershire sauce. Micro on **High 6 Minutes,** until cheese melts.

1 egg, beaten

2. Add egg and Micro on **High 2 Minutes.**

1 can (3 oz.) French Fried
 Onion Rings

3. Crush onion rings and mix into cheese mixture. Serve on toast or party crackers.

DIPSY DEVIL DIP

Utensils: 2 quart dish
Time: 2 minutes
Servings: 10

1 jar pimiento cheese spread
1 can deviled ham
1/4 cup mayonnaise
2 tablespoons parsley,
 chopped
1 teaspoon onion, grated
4 drops hot sauce

1. In 2 quart dish, put cheese. Micro on **High 2 Minutes.** Add remaining ingredients. Mix well. Serve with raw vegetables such as cauliflower, carrots, cucumbers, bell pepper.

5

HOT CHEESE CRACKERS

Utensils: Small dish
              Round platter
Time: 6 minutes
Servings: 15

3 oz. package cream cheese

1. In small dish, put cream cheese. Micro on **High 3 Minutes.**

1 tablespoon green onions, chopped
1/4 cup mayonnaise
1 tablespoon chives
1/8 teaspoon cayenne pepper
1/8 cup Parmesan cheese

2. Add all other ingredients. Mix well. Spoon on party crackers. Place on platter. Micro on **High 3 Minutes** until puffy.

MARINATED PARTY VEGETABLES

Utensils: 3 quart deep dish
              Deep salad bowl
Time: 7-8 minutes
Servings: 20-30

2 cups olive oil
3 cups wine vinegar
4 teaspoons salt
2 teaspoons pepper
1/2 cup sugar
2 cloves garlic

1. In 3 quart dish, combine all ingredients. Micro on **High** about **7-8 Minutes,** until boiling. Cool for 8 minutes and add raw vegetables. Marinate for 24 hours. Pour off most of marinade before serving.

Raw vegetables:
carrots - sliced
radishes
bell pepper - cut in strips
celery - cut in 1 inch pieces
zucchini - sliced
black olives
small onions
cauliflower - broken into pieces
mushrooms - raw or
           canned buttons

MARINATED VEGETABLES

Utensils: 2 quart dish or casserole
Time: 31 minutes
Servings: 20-30

**1 package (10 oz.) frozen
cauliflower or 1 head
cauliflower
1/4 cup water**

1. In 2 quart dish, put cauliflower and water. Micro on **High 7 Minutes, Covered.** If fresh cauliflower is used, Micro on **High 10 Minutes, Covered.** Drain.

**1 box or bag frozen carrots
1/4 cup water**

2. In 2 quart dish, put carrots and water. Micro on **High 7 Minutes, Covered.** Drain.

**1 box (10 oz.) frozen broccoli
spears
1/4 cup water**

3. In 2 quart dish, put broccoli and water. Micro on **High 7 Minutes, Covered.** Drain.

**1 can (any size) mushroom
buttons, drained
1 or 2 bottles (16 oz.) Italian
Salad Dressing**

4. In a large dish, put drained cauliflower, carrots, broccoli and mushrooms. Pour salad dressing over all, making sure dressing covers vegetables well. Place in refrigerator overnight to marinate. Serve in dressing or remove from dressing and arrange on serving platter.

RAW VEGETABLE DIP

Utensils: 2 quart dish
Time: 1 minute
Servings: 10

12 oz. package cream cheese
2 tablespoons onion, minced

1. In 2 quart dish, put cream cheese and onion. Mix. Micro on **High 1 Minutes.** Mix well.

1 carton (8 oz.) sour cream
2 tablespoons ketchup
1/4 teaspoon garlic powder
1 teaspoon lemon juice
— dash salt
— dash pepper
— dash of hot sauce

2. Add sour cream, ketchup, garlic powder, lemon juice, salt, pepper and hot sauce. Mix well. Serve with fresh vegetables.

   carrots - cut in sticks
   celery - cut in bite size sticks
   cherry tomatoes - cut in half
   cucumbers - sliced
   radishes - whole
   broccoli - uncooked in pieces
   cauliflower - uncooked in pieces
   shrimp - boiled and peeled

   Arrange vegetables on platter with vegetable dip in the center.

CRAB DIP

Utensils: 3 quart casserole
Time: 14 minutes
Servings: 15-20

1 block oleo or (8 tablespoons)
1 cup onion, chopped fine
1/2 cup celery, chopped fine

1. In 3 quart casserole, put oleo, onion and celery. Micro on **High 5 Minutes,** until completely sauteed.

1/2 cup flour
1/2 teaspoon cayenne pepper
1/2 teaspoon black pepper
— dash garlic powder
1 tablespoon salt

2. Add flour, pepper, garlic powder and salt. Stir well.

1 cup evaporated milk

3. Stir in evaporated milk slowly. Micro on **70% Power 4 Minutes** until thick, stirring once or twice.

1 pound white lump crabmeat

4. Stir in crabmeat. Micro on **High 5 Minutes,** stirring to keep smooth. If mixture is too thick, add a little more milk.

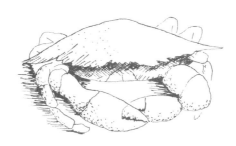

SHRIMP OR CRAB DIP I

Utensils: 3 quart casserole dish
Time: 11 minutes
Servings: 15-20

8 tablespoons butter
1/2 cup onion, chopped
1/2 cup green onions, chopped

1. In 3 quart dish, put butter, onion and green onions. Micro on **High 4 Minutes.**

1/2 cup all purpose flour
1 large can (13 oz.) evaporated milk
2 pounds shrimp, boiled, peeled and chopped or
1 pound of white lump crabmeat
1/4 cup parsley, chopped
1/2 pound Cheddar cheese, grated or chopped small
salt and pepper to taste
— dash of garlic powder

2. Add flour. Stir. Add evaporated milk gradually, stirring. Add shrimp or crabmeat (or both). Add parsley, cheese, salt, pepper and garlic powder. Micro on **High 6-7 Minutes,** until cheese melts and thickens. Serve hot with party crackers.

NOTE: Can be served in baked patty shells.

SHRIMP OR CRAB DIP II

Utensils: 2 quart casserole or dish
Time: 6 minutes
Servings: 15

8 oz. package cream cheese

1. In 2 quart dish, Micro cream cheese until slightly soft.

1 pound crabmeat or
1-1/2 pound shrimp, boiled, peeled and chopped fine
1/4 cup mayonnaise
1/2 cup onion, chopped fine or put in food processor
1/4 teaspoon garlic powder
salt and pepper to taste
— dash hot sauce
Worcestershire sauce to taste

2. To cream cheese, add crabmeat or shrimp, mayonnaise, onion, garlic powder, salt, pepper, hot sauce and Worcestershire sauce. Mix well. Micro on **High 6 Minutes,** or serve cold. Serve with party crackers.

CRAWFISH DIP

Utensils: 3 quart dish or casserole
Time: 9 minutes
Servings: 10-15

1 block oleo
1/2 cup green onions, chopped

1. In 3 quart dish, put oleo and green onions. Micro on **High 4 Minutes.** Stir.

1 pound boiled crawfish, chopped small

2. Add crawfish. Micro on **High 3 Minutes.** Stir.

1/4 cup flour
1 can (4 oz.) mushroom pieces and liquid
1/4 cup water
salt and pepper to taste
hot sauce to taste
1 teaspoon Worcestershire sauce

3. Add flour. Stir. Add mushrooms and liquid, salt, pepper and Worcestershire sauce. Micro on **70% Power 2-3 Minutes,** until thickened. Stir once or twice while cooking.

1 carton (8 oz.) sour cream

4. Stir in sour cream. Serve immediately with party crackers.

Soups
Gumbos

SOUPS

Cajun Oyster Soup 14

Creamy Oyster Soup 15

Green Thumb Soup 16

Onion Soup 17

Vegetable Soup 18

GUMBOS

Chicken Okra Gumbo 19

Seafood Gumbo 20

Shrimp Okra Gumbo 21

"Re-discover the family being together. Let dinner-time be a time of fun and laughter, a time of music and conversation, serious and gay."

CAJUN OYSTER SOUP

Utensils: 4 cup glass measuring cup
          4 quart Corning dish or similar dish
Time: 42 minutes
Servings: 8

1/2 cup oil
1-1/2 cups onion, chopped

1. In 4 cup glass measuring cup, put oil and onion. Micro on **High 5 Minutes.**

1/2 cup green pepper, chopped
1/2 cup celery, chopped
1/4 cup onion whites, chopped
1 large tomato, chopped

2. Add green pepper, celery, onion whites and tomato. Micro on **High 7 Minutes.**

1 pint oyster liquid
1/2 cup green onions, chopped
1/2 cup parsley, chopped
1/2 tablespoon basil
2-1/2 tablespoons salt
1/2 teaspoon cayenne pepper
— dash black pepper
1/4 teaspoon garlic powder

3. Add oyster liquid, green onions, parsley, basil, salt, pepper and garlic powder. Micro on **70% Power 5 Minutes.**

1 pint oysters
4 cups very hot water

4. Add oysters and water. Micro on **50% Power 10 Minutes,** then on **High 10 Minutes.**

1 cup vermicelli, crushed
1/2 teaspoon file'

5. Add vermicelli. Micro on **High 5 Minutes.** Sprinkle with file'. If more salt or pepper is needed, add to taste.

CREAMY OYSTER SOUP

Utensils: 2-1/2 quart dish
Time: 14 minutes
Servings: 4-6

3 tablespoons oleo
3 tablespoons green onions, chopped

1. In 2-1/2 quart dish, put oleo and green onions. Micro on **High 3 Minutes.**

2-1/2 cups chicken broth
1 pint oysters, drained and chopped, (reserve liquid)

2. Add chicken broth and oyster liquid. Micro on **High 3 Minutes.** If cold chicken broth is used, micro chicken broth and oyster liquid on **High 8 Minutes** instead of **3 Minutes.** Add chopped oysters. Micro on **High 3 Minutes.**

4 egg yolks, slightly beaten
1 cup half and half or 1/2 cup evaporated milk plus 1/2 cup milk
2 tablespoons chives
2 tablespoons parsley, chopped
2/3 teaspoon salt
1/4 teaspoon cayenne pepper

3. In small dish, add half and half or milk to beaten egg yolks. Add some hot chicken broth mixture to egg-milk mixture; whisk or stir slowly. Add to chicken broth mixture, stirring slowly. Add chives, parsley, salt and pepper. Micro on **70% Power 5 Minutes,** stirring occasionally. Do not boil. Serve hot.

GREEN THUMB SOUP

Utensils: 2-1/2 to 3 quart dish or 8 cup batter bowl
Time: 12 minutes
Servings: 6

2 tablespoons oleo
1/2 cup onion, chopped

1. In 2-1/2 to 3 quart dish or 8 cup batter bowl, put oleo and onion. Micro on **High 4 Minutes.**

4 cups chicken broth
1/4 cup bottled Italian
Salad Dressing
*2 cups cooked chicken, cut in
chunks (optional) (see
cooked chicken) or 2
cups cooked sausage,
cut in pieces (optional)
1-1/2 cups mixed salad greens,
torn in pieces (spinach,
lettuce, celery, green
pepper, etc.)
1-1/4 teaspoons salt
1/4 teaspoon black pepper
1/2 teaspoon cayenne pepper

2. Add chicken broth, salad dressing, chicken or sausage, salad greens, salt and pepper. Micro on **70% Power 8 Minutes,** or until hot. Serve with warm garlic bread.

NOTE: You may add a dash of file' to soup.

*NOTE: Use 4 cups of water to cook chicken for this recipe. Two cups of cooked chicken is approximately one 2 to 3 pound chicken.

ONION SOUP

Utensils: 3 quart dish
Time: 23 minutes
Servings: 8

**3 medium onions, sliced
    thinly
5 tablespoons oleo**

1. In 3 quart dish, put onion and oleo. Micro on **High 13 Minutes, Covered** with glass lid or plastic wrap. Stir once during cooking.

**1 tablespoon flour
1 teaspoon Worcestershire
    sauce
2 cans (10-1/2 oz.) beef broth
1/4 teaspoon cayenne pepper
1/4 teaspoon black pepper
1/4 teaspoon salt
1 cup hot water
Parmesan cheese
croutons**

2. Stir in flour. Add Worcestershire sauce, beef broth, pepper, salt and water. Micro on **High 10 Minutes.** Sprinkle with cheese and croutons.

VEGETABLE SOUP

Utensils: 5 quart dish
Time: 60 minutes
Servings: 6

1 cup water
2/3 cup cabbage, chopped
1 carrot, chopped small
2 small potatoes, cut small

1. In 5 quart dish, put water, cabbage, carrots and potatoes. Cover and Micro on **High 10 Minutes.**

2 quarts hot water
1-1/2 pounds of beef meat
　　or soup meat
1 large onion, chopped
1 stalk of celery, chopped
1/2 green pepper, chopped
2/3 cup green onions, chopped
1/2 cup tomato paste
1 bay leaf
— dash of oregano
1/4 teaspoon garlic powder
1/2 teaspoon black pepper
1/2 teaspoon cayenne pepper
2 teaspoons salt
1/4 cup parsley, chopped

2. Add two quarts of water, meat, onion, celery, green pepper, green onions, tomato paste, bay leaf, oregano, garlic powder, pepper, salt and parsley. Micro on **High 35 Minutes, Covered.** Stir during cooking.

1 can (16 oz.) mixed vegetables

3. Add can of vegetables. Uncover and Micro on **High 15 Minutes.**

CHICKEN OKRA GUMBO

Utensils: 4 or 5 quart casserole dish
            4 cup measuring cup (glass)
Time: 71 minutes
Servings: 6 to 8

1/2 cup oil
2-1/2 to 3 cups fresh okra,
   chopped, or
1 package frozen okra
   (defrosted)

1. In 4 or 5 quart dish, put okra and oil. Micro on **High 20 Minutes, Uncovered.** Set aside.

2/3 cup oil
2/3 cup flour

2. Roux: In 4 cup measuring cup, put oil and flour. Micro on **High 7-8 Minutes,** stirring at about **6-1/2 Minutes,** (just when Roux is starting to darken). Micro Roux until golden brown.

1 cup onion, chopped
1/4 cup green onions, chopped

3. Add onion and green onions to Roux. Micro on **High 3 Minutes.**

1 chicken, raw and cut or 6-8
   meaty parts
1/4 cup fresh parsley, chopped
   or 2 tablespoons parsley
   flakes
1/4 cup green bell pepper,
   chopped or pepper flakes
   (2 tablespoons)

4. Add Roux to okra mixture. Stir. Add raw chicken, parsley and bell pepper. Cover with lid or plastic wrap. Micro on **High 10 Minutes.** (Steam will smother chicken).

1 tablespoon salt
1 teaspoon cayenne pepper
1/2 teaspoon black pepper
1/4 teaspoon garlic powder
2 bay leaves
3 chicken bouillon cubes
1 can (16 oz.) whole tomatoes
1-1/2 quarts hot water

5. Add salt, pepper, garlic powder, bay leaf, chicken cubes and tomatoes. (Add tomatoes slowly, so temperature change won't break dish.) Add water slowly and stir in a little at the time. Micro on **High 30 Minutes, Uncovered.** Stir at intervals. Remove oil from top. Add dash of file'. Let stand 10 minutes. If more salt or pepper is needed, add to taste. If mixture seems too thick, add a little water.

SEAFOOD GUMBO

Utensils: 5 quart dish
　　　　　4 cup glass measuring cup
Time: 46 minutes
Servings: 8-10

2/3 cup oil
2/3 cup flour

1. Roux: In 4 cup measuring cup, put oil and flour. Micro on **High 7-9 Minutes,** until golden brown. Stir at about 6-1/2 minutes or just as roux is starting to brown, then again as roux darkens. (Roux will burn if not stirred as it starts to darken.)

1 cup onion, chopped
1/4 cup green pepper,
　　chopped

2. Add onion and green pepper. Micro on **High** about **3 Minutes,** until sauteed. Put mixture in 5 quart dish.

1/4 cup parsley, chopped or
　　2 tablespoons parsley
　　flakes
1/2 cup green onions, chopped
— dash garlic powder
2 teaspoons salt
1 teaspoon cayenne pepper
1/4 teaspoon black pepper
3 chicken bouillon cubes,
　　(optional)
1-1/2 quarts HOT water,
　　(6 cups)

3. Add parsley, green onions, garlic powder, salt, pepper, bouillon cubes and hot water. Micro on **High 10 Minutes, Covered** with lid or plastic wrap.

1-1/2 to 2 pounds shrimp, raw
　　and peeled
1 pound crab meat or 8-10 crab
　　halves, boiled and cleaned

4. Add shrimp and crabmeat. Micro on **High 10 Minutes, Uncovered.**

1 pint oysters and liquid
1 teaspoon file'

5. Add oysters. Micro on **High 10 Minutes, Uncovered,** then on **70% Power 5 Minutes, Uncovered.** Add file'. Let stand 10 minutes.

SHRIMP OKRA GUMBO

Utensils: 4 or 5 quart deep dish casserole
4 cup glass measuring cup
Time: 66 minutes
Servings: 8-10

1/2 cup oil
4-1/2 to 5 cups fresh okra, chopped or 2 packages frozen okra, defrosted

1. In 4 or 5 quart dish, put okra and oil. Micro on **High 25 Minutes, Uncovered.** Set aside.

2/3 cup oil
2/3 cup flour

2. Roux: In 4 cup measuring cup, put oil and flour. Micro on **High 7-1/2 to 8 Minutes,** or until dark brown. Stir at about 6-1/2 minutes just as Roux starts to darken (or Roux may burn).

1 cup onion, chopped
1/4 cup green onions, chopped

3. Add onion and green onions. Micro on **High 3 Minutes.**

2 pounds raw shrimp, peeled
1/4 cup fresh parsley, chopped or 1 tablespoon parsley flakes
3 bay leaves
1/4 cup green pepper, chopped or 2 tablespoons pepper flakes

4. Add shrimp, parsley, bay leaves, green pepper and Roux mixture to okra mixture. Stir. Cover with lid or plastic wrap. Micro on **High 10 Minutes.**

2 teaspoons salt
1 teaspoon cayenne pepper
1/2 teaspoon black pepper
— dash of garlic powder
3 chicken bouillon cubes
1 can (16 oz.) whole tomatoes
1-1/2 quarts very hot water (6 cups)
1/2 teaspoon file'

5. Uncover. Add salt, pepper, garlic powder, chicken cubes, tomatoes and water. (Add tomatoes and water very slowly, mixing in a little at a time, so heat change won't break bowl). Micro on **High 20 Minutes, Uncovered.** Stir at intervals. Add 1/2 teaspoon file'. If more salt or pepper is needed, add to taste. Remove oil from top with large spoon. Serve over rice.

NOTE: If a spicier gumbo is desired, use 1 can (10 oz.) Ro-Tel tomatoes in place of 16 oz. can of regular tomatoes. Omit pepper.

Meats
and
Meat Dishes

MEATS AND MEAT DISHES

Hints on Cooking Meat...................................... 24
Preparing Convenience Meats 25
Meat Defrosting 26
Barbecued Ribs... 27
Beef or Pork Roast....................................... 28
Brown Gravy for Roast 29
Beef Stew Country.. 30
Curried Shrimp or Ground Beef 31
Barbecued Sausage or Chicken Spaghetti................. 32
Fresh Sausage with/without Wine Sauce 33
Chili and Bean Enchilada Casserole 34
Chili and Beans... 35
Cowboy Annie's Beer Chili 36
Hot Dog Chili... 37
Dirty Rice Dressing 38
French Oyster Dressing 39
Baked Ham.. 40
Hot Ham Sandwich 41
Ham and Cheese Meatloaf 42
Hamburgers 43
Lasagna 44
Lasagna II 44, 45
Mazetti 46
Barbecued Pork Chops 47
Breaded Pork Chops...................................... 48
Pork Chops in Brown Gravy 48
Stuffed Green Peppers 49

*"There is nothing a woman
cannot achieve, if she has the
courage to try it."*

MEAT

1. Cooking times of meats may vary depending on **Weight, Shape, Size, Amount of Fat** and whether they are **Tender Cuts** or **Less Tender Cuts** of meat.

2. Meat should be **Placed in a Shallow Baking Dish** on a roasting rack or trivet.

3. Meat should be **Placed Fat Side Down To Start** and turned over half of cooking time.

4. Meat may be **Covered Lightly** with **Wax Paper** or **Paper Towels** to prevent splatter.

5. Meat **May Be Cooked in Roasting Bags.** Tie the bag with string instead of metal tie. Make slit in bag.

6. **Do Not Salt Meat Before Cooking.** Salt draws out moisture and toughens outer layer of meat. You may dissolve salt in water and rub on meat before cooking.

7. **Micro-Shake,** a new browning agent or seasoning is now available for purchase and can be used on smaller cuts of meat which don't cook long enough to brown. Micro-Shake browns meat beautifully and gives chicken a golden crust. Meats cooked longer than 10 minutes will brown on their own.

8. Meat continues to cook after taken from oven. It should **Stand 10 to 15 Minutes** before serving.

9. A **Browning Dish May Be Used** to brown meat before cooking or meat may be browned on range top.

10. **Defrost Meat Completely** before cooking.

11. **Tender Cuts** of meat may be cooked on **High or 70% Power.** If you prefer, you may even cook on 50% power. See chart for time and temperature.

12. **Less Tender Cuts** of meat should be **Cooked More Slowly** to become tender. See chart for cuts of meat.

13. **Less Tender Cuts** of meat should be **Cooked in Their Juices** and cooked **Covered.**

14. Meats should be **Turned Over Half Way of Cooking Time.**

15. Some less tender cuts of meat are: Chuck and Rump.

PREPARING CONVENIENCE MEATS

ITEM	Amount	Power Select	Approx. Heat. Time (in minutes)	Standing Time (in minutes)
Beef Patties, frozen	1	High	2½ to 3	2
(3½ oz. ea.)	2		3½ to 4½	3
	4		5½ to 6½	3
Bacon, slices		High	45 sec. to 1 min. per strip	1
Canadian Bacon, slices		High	45 sec. to 1 min. per strip	3
Frankfurters, scored	2	High	1½ to 2	3
	4		2½ to 3½	3
Hot Dog, on Bun	1	High	30-45 sec.	
Ham, slices	2	High	1½ to 2½	3
(about 2 oz. ea.)	4		2½ to 3½	3
Hamburgers	1	High	¾ to 1¼	2
(4 oz. ea.)	2		1½ to 2	2
	4		3½ to 4	2
Sausage Links, frozen	2	High	1 to 1½	2
(precooked, brown	4		1½ to 2	2
and serve)	8		3 to 4	2
Sausage Links, fresh	2	High	2 to 3	3
(1 to 2 oz. ea.)	4		4 to 5	3
	8		6½ to 7½	3
Sausage Patties, fresh	2	High	1 to 2½	2
(1 to 2 oz. ea.)	4		2 to 4	2
Ground Meat (to brown for casserole)	1 lb.	High or 70% Power	8 to 10	
Meat Loaf	1 lb.	High	13	
	2 lb.		18 to 20	

MEAT DEFROSTING CHART

CUT	Approximate Time Per Pound
Ground Beef	8 min.
Hamburger Patties	8 - 9 min.
Steak 3/4" Thick	7 - 8 min.
Chops	8 min.
Ribs	6 min.
Roasts: Beef, Pork, Veal, Lamb	8 - 10 min.

Your Own Notes ...

BARBECUED RIBS

Utensils: 4 quart Corning dish or
            Clay Simmer Pot
Time: 40 minutes
Servings: 6

2 to 3 pounds short ribs
1 cup onion, chopped
1/4 cup green onions,
    chopped
1/2 cup celery, chopped
1 tablespoon mustard
1 teaspoon salt
1/2 teaspoon cayenne pepper
2 tablespoons brown sugar
1/4 cup cooking wine
    (optional)
1 tablespoon Worcestershire
    sauce
1/4 cup wine vinegar
1 cup tomato ketchup

1. In 4 quart dish or Simmer Pot, put all ingredients. Micro on **High 15 Minutes, Covered.** Rearrange ribs. Re-cover and Micro on **50% Power 55-60 Minutes.** Let stand 15 minutes. Skim off excess fat.

NOTE: Chicken (cut up) may be substituted in place of ribs. Micro chicken on **High 30 Minutes, Covered.** Uncover last 5 minutes of cooking.

NOTE: Either pork or beef ribs may be used.

NOTE: If Simmer Pot is used, soak pot and cover in water 15 minutes before using.

27

BEEF OR PORK ROAST

Season roast with garlic powder, pepper, Kitchen Bouquet or onion soup mix. Place fat side down on roasting rack in 4 quart Corning dish or clay simmer pot. Cover with wax paper, or put in browning bag. (Make slits in bag.) Turn roast over half way during cooking time. Insert temperature probe or microwave thermometer about half way of cooking time. Follow chart below:

RIB ROAST

APPROXIMATE TIME	Power Setting	Temp. At End Of Cooking	Temp. At End Of Standing
12 minutes per pound, rare	50%	120-130°	130-140° F
14 minutes per pound, medium	50%	140-150° F	150-160° F
16 minutes per pound, well done	50%	160-165° F	170-175° F

NOTE: Let stand 15-20 minutes covered with foil.

CHUCK OR RUMP ROAST

20-23 minutes per pound	50%	155-165° F	165-175° F

NOTE: Cover chuck or rump with lid the entire cooking time.

PORK ROAST

18-22 minutes per pound	50%	170-175° F	175-185° F

BROWN GRAVY FOR ROAST

Utensils: Small mixing bowl

Cooked roast, sliced
1 can (10 oz.) Franco American
Beef Gravy
3 tablespoons flour
1 can (4 oz.) mushrooms and
liquid
1 teaspoon Kitchen Bouquet

1. In small bowl, mix all ingredients except roast. Put roast in 4 quart dish or similar dish. Pour gravy over roast. Micro on **70% Power** until gravy is thick as desired.

BEEF STEW COUNTRY

Utensils: 3 quart deep dish (Corning or Pyrex) or Clay Simmer Pot
Time: 73 minutes
Servings: 6

1/2 cup oil
1/2 cup flour

1. Roux: In 3 quart dish, put oil and flour. Micro on **High about 8 Minutes,** until golden brown. Stir at about 7 minutes or right as roux is turning brown in order to prevent burning.

2/3 cup onion, chopped
1/2 cup celery, chopped

2. Add onion and celery. Micro on **High 3 Minutes.**

1/4 cup green onions, chopped
1 pound beef stew meat,
    chopped in small chunks

3. Add green onions and stew meat. Micro on **High 7 Minutes, Covered** with lid or plastic wrap.

1/4 cup parsley, chopped or
    1 tablespoon parsley flakes
1-1/2 teaspoons salt
1/2 teaspoon black pepper
1/3 teaspoon cayenne pepper
— dash garlic powder
1 bay leaf
1/2 teaspoon Kitchen Bouquet
    (optional)
1 can (10 oz.) Franco-American
    beef gravy
2-1/4 cups hot water

4. Add parsley, salt, pepper, garlic powder, bay leaf, Kitchen Bouquet, beef gravy and hot water. Micro on **High 10 Minutes, Covered.** Micro on **50% Power 35 Minutes, Covered** with lid or plastic wrap. Micro on **High 10 Minutes, Uncovered,** or until thick.

NOTE: If you have a clay simmer pot, you may transfer ingredients to clay pot for Step 3 and continue to Step 4. Be sure to soak Simmer Pot and lid in water for 15 minutes before using.

CURRIED SHRIMP OR GROUND BEEF

Utensils: 3 quart casserole and lid or plastic wrap
7" by 11" oblong or 4 quart casserole
Time: 36 minutes
Servings: 8-10

1/4 cup oil
1-1/2 cups onion, chopped
1 cup green pepper, chopped

1. In 3 quart casserole, put oil, onion and green pepper. Micro on **High 13 Minutes, Uncovered** or until vegetables are very tender. Stir once during cooking.

1-1/2 pounds raw shrimp,
 peeled and chopped or
 1-1/2 pounds ground beef

2. Add shrimp and Micro on **High 5 Minutes.** If ground beef is used, Micro on **High 10 Minutes, Covered.** (Discard some juice).

2 cans (10 oz.) whole tomatoes
2-1/2 teaspoons salt
1/2 teaspoon cayenne pepper
1/4 teaspoon garlic powder
1 tablespoon curry powder

3. Add tomatoes, mashed. Add salt, pepper, garlic powder and curry powder. (If using ground beef, add 1 teaspoon chili powder.) Micro on **High 5 Minutes, Covered.**

3 cups cooked rice
1 cup Cheddar cheese, grated

4. Add cooked rice. (If still very juicy, Micro on **High 3 More Minutes, Uncovered.)** Put in baking dish or casserole. Top with cheese. Micro on **High 5 Minutes, Uncovered.**

BARBECUED SAUSAGE OR CHICKEN SPAGHETTI

Utensils: 4 quart Corning dish
4 cup glass measuring cup
Time: 68 minutes
Servings: 10

2 to 3 pounds fresh pork or beef sausage
1/2 cup oleo

1. In 4 quart Corning dish, put oleo. On top of range, heat slightly. Add sausage. Brown sausage well on both sides. Use a splatter screen since oleo heated in Corning dish on range top tends to splatter. Remove sausage and slice into bite size pieces. Set sausage aside.

1 cup onion, chopped
1 cup green bell pepper, chopped
1/4 cup green onions, whites only, chopped
1/2 teaspoon garlic powder

2. In 4 cup measuring cup, put sausage drippings, onion, green pepper, onion whites and garlic powder. Micro on **High 8 Minutes, Uncovered,** stirring.

1 can (10-3/4 oz.) cream of celery soup
1 can (10-3/4 oz.) cream of mushroom soup
1 can (10 oz.) Ro-Tel tomatoes
1 small can (5-3/4 oz.) mushroom steak sauce
1 can (4 oz.) mushroom pieces and liquid
1 cup barbecue sauce
1 can (8 oz.) tomato sauce
1 can (6 oz.) tomato paste
1 cup water

3. Add celery soup, mushroom soup, tomatoes, steak sauce, mushroom pieces and liquid, barbecue sauce, tomato sauce, tomato paste and water. Micro on **High 45 Minutes, Covered,** stirring.

1/2 cup green onions, chopped
1/2 cup parsley, chopped or 1/4 cup parsley flakes
1/2 teaspoon salt

4. Add sausage, green onions, parsley and salt. Micro on **70% Power 15 Minutes, Covered,** stirring.
Serve over rice, noodles, with french bread or as an hors d'oeuvre.

NOTE: Regular tomatoes may be substituted in place of Ro Tel tomatoes if a less spicy taste is desired.
NOTE: Chicken may be used in place of sausage. If it is, then do not brown chicken. Add chicken after water and continue Step 3.

FRESH SAUSAGE
WITH / WITHOUT WINE SAUCE

Utensils: 4 quart Corning dish
Time: 13 minutes
Servings: 6-8

1/4 cup oil
1 to 1-1/2 pounds fresh
sausage

1. In 4 quart Corning dish, brown sausage in oil on top of range. Remove sausage and set aside.

1/2 cup onion, chopped
1/4 cup green bell pepper,
chopped, or 1 tablespoon
pepper flakes

2. To oil in 4 quart dish, put onion and green pepper. Micro on **High 3-4 Minutes,** until sauteed. Drain off oil.

1/2 tablespoon Kitchen
Bouquet
1 tablespoon flour
1 teaspoon A-1 Steak Sauce
(optional)
2 tablespoons Marsala wine or
any cooking wine
1 teaspoon parsley flakes
3/4 cup hot water
1/2 teaspoon cayenne pepper
1/2 teaspoon salt

3. Add sausage, Kitchen Bouquet, flour, Steak Sauce, wine, parsley flakes, water, salt and pepper. Stir. Micro on **High 10 Minutes, Covered** with lid. Rearrange once during cooking.

NOTE: Wine may be omitted if desired, or less may be used.

CHILI AND BEAN ENCHILADA CASSEROLE

Utensils: 2-1/2 to 3 quart dish
            7" x 11" oblong casserole
Time: 24 minutes
Servings: 8

3 tablespoons oleo **1/2 cup onion, chopped**	1. In 2 to 3 quart dish, put oleo and onion. Micro on **High 3 Minutes.**
1 pound lean ground beef	2. Add ground beef. Micro on **High 5 Minutes,** stirring to break up beef. (A potato masher is excellent to separate meat.)
1 package Chili Seasoning Mix **1 can (8 oz.) tomato sauce** **2/3 cup water** **1 can (1 pound) Kidney beans** **(not cream style)** **1/2 teaspoon pepper** **salt to taste**	3. Add Chili mix, tomato sauce, water, kidney beans, pepper and salt. Micro on **High 8 Minutes, Covered** with wax paper.
1 package (12) tortillas **1-1/2 cups Cheddar cheese,** **grated** **2 cups lettuce, shredded**	4. Pass each tortilla quickly through warm water. In 7" x 11" oblong dish, layer 3 tortillas, then 1/3 bean-chili mixture, then 1/3 cheese, then 1/3 lettuce. Repeat with next 3 tortillas, etc. Micro on **High 8-11 Minutes,** until heated through and is tender in middle.

CHILI AND BEANS

Utensils: 3 or 4 quart Corning (or similar) dish
Time: 38 minutes
Servings: 6-8

3 tablespoons oil
2/3 cup onion, chopped
1/4 cup green pepper,
   chopped

1.   In 3 or 4 quart dish, put oil, onion and green pepper. Micro on **High 5 Minutes.**

1 pound ground beef

2.   Add ground beef. Mash with potato masher to separate. Micro on **High 8-9 Minutes,** stirring and mashing once or twice with potato masher to separate.

1 can (10 oz.) whole tomatoes
1 can (6 oz.) tomato paste
— dash garlic powder
2 tablespoons chili powder
1/2 bay leaf
1-1/4 teaspoons salt
— dash powdered cloves or
   3 whole cloves
1/8 teaspoon cayenne pepper
1/4 teaspoon oregano
   (optional)

3.   Add tomatoes, tomato paste, garlic powder, chili powder, bay leaf, salt, cloves, pepper and oregano. Micro on **High 20 Minutes, Covered,** stirring once or twice.

1 can (15 oz.) Kidney beans
(not creamed style)

4.   Add beans. Micro on **High 5 Minutes.**

NOTE: This recipe can be doubled for a large crowd. If so use the following times: Step 1.   8 minutes
                                                    Step 2.   15 minutes
                                                    Step 3.   28 minutes
                                                    Step 4.   8 minutes

MEAT

COWBOY ANNIE'S BEER CHILI

Utensils: 4 quart Corning or pyrex dish
Time: 35 minutes
Servings: 8

1 cup onion, chopped
1/2 cup green onions,
    chopped
1/4 cup celery, chopped
1/4 cup oil

1.   In 4 quart dish, put onion, green onions, celery and oil. Micro on **High 5 Minutes, Uncovered.**

2 pounds ground beef

2.   Add beef and Micro on **High 10 Minutes,** stirring and mashing beef at intervals.

1 can (10 oz.) whole tomatoes
1 can (8 oz.) tomato sauce
1 can (6 oz.) tomato paste
2 bay leaves
2 tablespoons flour
4 tablespoons chili powder
1/2 to 3/4 cup beer
1/2 teaspoon sweet basil
1-1/2 teaspoons salt
1/2 teaspoon cayenne pepper
1/2 tablespoon sugar

3.   Add all remaining ingredients and Micro on **High 20 Minutes, Covered.** Discard oil which may settle on top. Stir once or twice during cooking.

NOTE: Recipe may be cut in half. If so, divide all ingredients in half except tomatoes, tomato sauce and tomato paste. Use a 3 quart dish. Cook **beef 7 minutes instead of 10 minutes** and cook **remaining ingredients 15 minutes instead of 20 minutes.**

HOT DOG CHILI

Utensils: 3 quart dish
Time: 39 minutes
Servings: 6-8

2 tablespoons oil
1/2 cup onion, chopped
1/4 cup green pepper, chopped

1. In 3 quart dish, put oil, onion and green pepper. Micro on **High 6 Minutes.** Stir to prevent sticking.

1 pound ground beef

2. Add beef. Mash to break up. Micro on **High 8 Minutes, Stirring and Mashing** to prevent lumping.

1 tablespoon flour
2 tablespoons chili powder
1 teaspoon salt
1 teaspoon sugar
pepper to taste
2 cans (8 oz.) tomato sauce
1 cup water

3. Stir in flour, chili, salt, sugar and pepper. Mix well. Add tomato sauce and water. Micro on **High 5 Minutes, Covered** with wax paper. Micro on **70% Power 20 Minutes, Covered** with wax paper to prevent splatter. Stir a least twice during cooking.

DIRTY RICE DRESSING

Utensils: 3 quart casserole and lid
Time: 44 minutes
Servings: 6

3 tablespoons oil
1 cup onion, chopped
1/2 cup green pepper,
     chopped
1/4 cup celery, chopped
1/4 cup green onions, chopped
1/4 cup parsley, chopped

1. In 3 quart dish, put oil, onion, green pepper, celery, green onions and parsley. Micro on **High 8 Minutes.**

1 pound lean ground beef

2. Add beef. Micro on **High 6 Minutes, Covered.** Drain off fat.

1-1/4 cups Minute rice
1 can (10 oz.) onion soup
1 can (10 oz.) cream of chicken
     soup
1 teaspoon salt
1/4 teaspoon garlic powder
1/2 teaspoon cayenne pepper
1/4 teaspoon black pepper

3. Add rice, soups, salt, garlic powder and pepper. Micro on **50% Power 10 Minutes, Covered.** Stir. Micro on **50% Power 10 More Minutes, Covered.** Then Micro on **50% Power 10 Minutes, Uncovered.** Let stand 10 minutes.

NOTE: Last 10 minutes, 1 can (4 oz.) mushroom pieces (drained) may be added.

FRENCH OYSTER DRESSING

Utensils: 4 quart casserole
4 cup measuring cup
Time: 56 minutes
Servings: 10-12

1/4 cup oil
1 cup onion, chopped
2/3 cup green onions, chopped
1/2 cup celery, chopped
1/4 cup green pepper,
  chopped

1.   In 4 cup measuring cup, put oil, green onions, celery and green pepper. Micro on **High 8 Minutes, Uncovered.** Put in 4 quart casserole.

2 pounds lean ground beef
1 pound ground pork
1/4 cup parsley, chopped
1/2 can (10-3/4 oz.) cream of
  mushroom soup

2.   Add beef, pork, parsley and soup. Mash mixture with potato masher to keep from lumping. Micro on **High 25 Minutes, Covered.** Stir occasionally.

1 teaspoon black pepper
1-1/4 teaspoons cayenne
  pepper
1-1/4 teaspoons salt
1/2 pint (10-12) oysters and
  1/2 of juice

3.   Add pepper, salt, oysters and half of juice. Mash oysters into meat mixture. Micro on **70% Power 15 Minutes, Uncovered,** stirring occasionally.

1/2 cup Italian bread crumbs
4 slices bread, toasted
— dash garlic powder

4.   With large spoon, discard oil and some juices. Add bread crumbs, bread and garlic powder. Mash and blend thoroughly. Micro on **High 8 Minutes, Uncovered,** stirring and mixing occasionally.

NOTE: If a drier dressing is desired, add more bread crumbs. If a more spicy taste is desired, add more salt, pepper and garlic powder.

BAKED HAM
All Pre-Cooked or Fully Cooked Ham

Such as:
- Boneless Ham
- Canned Ham
- Cured Ham (Pork Shoulder)
- Southern Type Ham
- Bone-in-Ham

COOKING TIME	Power Setting	Temp. At End Of Cooking	Temp. At End Standing Time
5-6 minutes per pound	70% Power	120° F	130° F

DIRECTIONS:
   Place ham fat-side down on microwave roasting rack in 4 quart dish or similar (9" x 13"). Cover with plastic wrap or place in browning bag on roasting rack. Turn over half way during cooking time. Insert temperature probe or a microwave thermometer about 15 minutes before end of cooking time and add glaze. Remove ham at 120° F, and let stand until it reaches 130° F (about 15 minutes), covered with foil.

All Fresh Hams or Uncooked Hams

METHOD I:

COOKING TIME	Power Setting	Temp. At End Of Cooking	Temp At End Standing Time
12 minutes per pound	70% Power	170-175° F	180-185° F

METHOD II:

16 minutes per pound	50% Power	170-175° F	180-185° F

DIRECTIONS:
   Use same cooking procedures as in Fully Cooked Hams.

GLAZE FOR HAM

1 can (8 oz.) pineapple slices, reserve juice
1/2 cup brown sugar
1 cup coca-cola

1. In small bowl, mix pineapple juice, brown sugar and coke. Pour over ham. Put pineapple slices on ham. Secure with toothpicks.

40

HOT HAM SANDWICH
(Delicious)

Utensils: Flat casserole dish to fit 4 large hamburger buns
                    Small bowl
Time: 4 minutes
Servings: 4

4 large hamburger buns
1 pound sliced ham
4 slices Cheddar cheese

1.   Put about 1/4 pound ham on each bun. Top with cheese slice. Top with 1 teaspoon Mustard Sauce (below). Place on flat casserole dish. Micro on **High 3-1/2 to 4 Minutes,** until cheese melts. Serve hot.

MUSTARD SAUCE

3 tablespoons oleo, melted
1-1/2 tablespoons mustard
1/2 tablespoon Worcestershire
    sauce
1 tablespoon onion, chopped
    fine or grated

2.   In small bowl, put oleo, mustard, Worcestershire sauce and onion. Mix well.

HAM AND CHEESE MEATLOAF

Utensils: Large mixing bowl
            7" x 11" oblong casserole
Time: 35 minutes
Servings: 6-8

2 pounds ground beef
1 egg, beaten
1 can (8 oz.) Ro-Tel tomatoes
1 cup Italian bread crumbs
1/4 teaspoon garlic powder
— dash pepper
1/2 teaspoon salt

1. In mixing bowl, mix ground beef, egg, tomatoes, bread crumbs, garlic powder, salt and pepper.

4 to 5 slices ham
1 small package Mozarella
    cheese, grated or
    6 slices American cheese

2. On a piece of wax paper, pat out ground beef mixture into the shape of a rectangle. Place slices of ham over ground beef, leaving a 1 inch border all around. Sprinkle with cheese, or cheese slices. Using wax paper to lift edge of beef, roll jelly roll fashion. Place in 7" x 11" casserole. Micro on **High 15 Minutes, Covered** with plastic wrap.

1 jar (15-1/2 oz.) Ragu
    spaghetti sauce

3. Uncover. Pour Ragu sauce over meat loaf and Micro on **High 20 Minutes,** covered with wax paper to prevent splatter. Remove and let stand covered with foil 10 minutes.

NOTE: This may be made into a regular meat loaf by omitting ham and cheese and just shape into a regular loaf.

HAMBURGERS

Utensils: 10" browning skillet or browning grill
2-3 quart mixing bowl
Time: 13 minutes
Servings: 4

1-1/2 pounds lean ground beef
3 teaspoons A-1 Steak Sauce
2/3 teaspoon black pepper
2/3 teaspoon cayenne pepper
1 teaspoon salt

1. In 2 or 3 quart mixing bowl, mix all ingredients. Shape into 4 patties. Preheat skillet or grill on **High 8 Minutes.** Place patties on skillet or grill. Micro on **High 3 Minutes, Covered** with wax paper. Turn patties over and Micro on **High 2 More Minutes, Covered** with wax paper.

NOTE: If you prefer another hamburger mixture, use your own and use the same cooking time and procedure as in step 1.

LASAGNA
(Quick and Easy)

Utensils: 2-1/2 to 3 quart dish
           Small bowl
           7" x 11" oblong casserole dish
Time: 30 minutes
Servings: 6

1 pound lean ground beef

1. In 2-1/2 to 3 quart dish, put ground beef. Micro on **High 7 Minutes.** Drain off fat.

1 jar (32 oz.) Ragu spaghetti sauce
1/4 cup water

2. Add Ragu sauce and water to ground beef. Micro on **High 5 Minutes.**

1 carton (12 oz.) cottage cheese
2 eggs
1/4 teaspoon black pepper
1/4 teaspoon cayenne pepper
1/2 teaspoon salt

3. In small bowl, mix cottage cheese, eggs, pepper and salt.

9 lasagne noodles, raw
2 cups Mozzarello cheese, grated
1/2 cup Parmesan cheese

4. In 7" x 11" oblong casserole, layer 1-1/2 cups tomato sauce, 3 lasagne noodles, 1/3 egg mixture, 3/4 cup Mozzarello cheese. Repeat two more times. (Reserve a little tomato sauce to top last layer of noodles.) Top with Parmesan cheese. Cover with double layer of plastic wrap. Micro on **High 8 Minutes,** then on **50% Power 30 Minutes** or until noodles are tender. Let stand 10-15 minutes.

LASAGNA II

Utensils: 7" x 11" oblong casserole
           4 quart Corning casserole or similar
           3 quart deep dish
Time: 52 minutes
Servings: 8-10

1 package (8 oz.) lasagna noodles
5 cups hot water
2 tablespoons oil
1 tablespoon salt

1. In 3 quart deep dish, put water, salt and oil. Bring to boil. Add lasagna. Cover and Micro on **High 15 Minutes** or until tender. Drain and rinse. Separate noodles before they stick together.

2 tablespoons oil 1 cup onion, chopped	2. In 4 quart casserole, put oil and onion. Micro on **High 5 Minutes,** stirring once or twice.
1 pound ground beef	3. Add beef and mash to separate. (A potato masher does a great job.) Micro on **High 7 Minutes,** stirring and mashing once or twice. Micro **Uncovered.**

2 cans (8 oz.) tomato sauce
1 can (6 oz.) tomato paste
1 can (10 oz) whole tomatoes
1-1/2 teaspoon basil
1/4 teaspoon garlic powder
1 tablespoon fresh parsley
    or flakes
1-1/2 teaspoons salt
1-1/2 teaspoons sugar
1/2 teaspoon cayenne pepper
1/2 teaspoon oregano
    (optional)
	4. Add tomato sauce, tomato paste, tomatoes, basil, garlic powder, parsley, salt, sugar, pepper and oregano. Stir. Micro on **High 10 Minutes, Covered** with lid. Stir occasionally during cooking.

1 carton (12 oz.) cottage cheese
2 eggs, beaten
1/2 teaspoon cayenne pepper
1/2 teaspoon black pepper
1 teaspoon salt
1 teaspoon salt
1 teaspoon parsley
1/3 cup Parmesan cheese

1 cup Mozzarella cheese,
    grated

5. In small bowl, mix cottage cheese, eggs, pepper, salt, parsley and Parmesan cheese. In oblong casserole put in layers as follows:

1/4 of noodles
1/4 of sauce
1/2 of cottage cheese
1/4 of noodles
1/4 of sauce
all of Mozzarella cheese
1/4 of noodles
1/4 of sauce
remainder of cottage cheese
1/4 of noodles
1/4 of sauce

Micro on **High 15 Minutes, Covered** with wax paper.

MAZETTI

Utensils: 10" Corning dish or Clay Simmer Pot
Small dish
Time: 42 minutes
Servings: 6

2 tablespoons oil
1 cup onion, chopped
1/3 cup green pepper, chopped
3/4 cup celery, chopped

1. In 10" dish or Simmer Pot, put oil, onion, green pepper and celery. Micro on **High 7-8 Minutes,** until tender. A smaller dish may be used to saute' these vegetables which would require less time but would soil an extra dish. Do as you prefer.

1 pound lean ground beef
1 package (5 oz.) small flat
egg noodles

2. Add ground beef. Mash with potato masher to separate. Micro on **High 7-8 Minutes, Uncovered,** until meat loses its red color. Mash and stir once or twice during cooking. Drain off fat. (Push meat and vegetables to outer part of dish while cooking, unless the dish used is small.) Sprinkle raw noodles on top.

2 cans (10 oz.) tomato soup,
undiluted
2 teaspoons salt
1/2 teaspoon chili powder
2/3 cup water
1 can (8 oz.) mushrooms,
drained (optional)
1/2 cup Cheddar cheese,
grated
pepper to taste

3. Mix together soup, salt, pepper, chili powder, water and mushrooms. Pour over noddles. Micro on **High 10 Minutes, Covered** with plastic wrap and a lid over plastic wrap. (This gives an intense steam effect.) Then Micro on **50% Power 15 Minutes.** Stir and sprinkle with cheese. Re-cover with lid only and Micro on **50% Power 3 Minutes.**

BARBECUED PORK CHOPS

Utensils: 4 quart Corning dish and lid
Time: 25 minutes
Servings: 6

3 tablespoons oil
6 pork chops

1. In 4 quart Corning dish, put oil and chops and fry on range top until slightly brown. Remove chops from 4 quart dish.

1 cup onion, chopped
1/2 cup celery, chopped

2. Add onion and celery. Micro on **High 5 Minutes.**

1/4 cup green onions, chopped
1 tablespoon mustard
1 teaspoon salt
1/2 teaspoon cayenne pepper
2 tablespoons brown sugar
1/8 cup (any type) cooking wine
1 teaspoon Worcestershire
**   sauce**
1/8 cup wine vinegar
1/2 cup tomato ketchup

3. Add chops, green onions, mustard, salt, pepper, sugar, wine, Worcestershire sauce, vinegar and tomato ketchup. Micro on **High 10 Minutes, Covered.** Then Micro on **High 5 Minutes, Uncovered.** Rearrange once during cooking.

BREADED PORK CHOPS

Utensils: Round roasting rack over glass pie dish or
            Oblong dish with oblong roasting rack
Time: 16 minutes (13 minutes per pound) at **70% Power**
Servings: 4

4 pork chops
1 egg, beaten
1 cup Italian bread crumbs
salt and pepper to taste

1. Season pork chops with salt and pepper. Dip in egg. Coat with bread crumbs. Place on roasting rack over pie dish. Micro on **70% Power 8 Minutes, Uncovered.** Turn pork chops over. Micro on **70% Power 8 more Minutes, Uncovered.** Cover with foil and let stand 8 minutes.

PORK CHOPS IN BROWN GRAVY

Utensils: 4 quart Corning casserole dish
Time: 10 minutes
Servings: 4-6

3 tablespoons butter or oleo
4-6 pork chops

1. In 4 quart dish, heat oleo on top of range until hot. Season pork chops with salt and pepper. In hot oleo, brown pork chops on both sides. (May need a splatter screen to cover since butter in a Corning dish on top of range tends to splatter.)

1 teaspoon flour
2 teaspoons Kitchen Bouquet
1/2 cup water
— dash garlic powder
1/2 teaspoon parsley flakes
— dash Worcestershire sauce

2. In small bowl, mix flour, Kitchen Bouquet, water, garlic powder, parsley flakes and Worcestershire sauce. Pour over chops. Cover with lid or plastic wrap. Micro on **70% Power 10 Minutes.** Let stand covered 10 minutes.

48

STUFFED GREEN PEPPERS

Utensils: Medium size mixing bowl
7" x 11" oblong casserole dish
Time: 25 minutes
Servings: 8

**4 medium green peppers,
    washed and halved**
1 pound lean ground beef
2/3 cup Italian bread crumbs
1 egg
1/2 cup tomato sauce
2 tablespoons water
3/4 teaspoon salt
1/2 teaspoon cayenne pepper
1/4 cup green pepper, chopped

1. In medium mixing bowl, mix beef, bread crumbs, egg, tomato sauce, water, salt, pepper and green pepper. Fill pepper halves with beef mixture.

1/2 can (8 oz.) tomato sauce
**1 jar (15-1/2 oz.) Ragu
    spaghetti sauce**

2. Pour tomato sauce and Ragu sauce over peppers. Cover with plastic wrap. Micro on **70% Power 25 Minutes.** Let stand 10 minutes.

49

Poultry

POULTRY

Poultry Hints 52
Poultry Defrosting 53
Poultry Roasting Chart 53
Roast Chicken 54
Roast Turkey 55
Cooked Chicken 56
Barbecued Chicken 56
Oven Crispy Chicken 57
Sweet and Sour Chicken 57
Chicken Enchilada Casserole 58
Chicken Stew.. 59
Cream of Chicken Quiche 60
Golden Chicken Souffle 61
Herbed Chicken 62
Hot Chicken Salad Casserole 63
Mandarin Chicken 64
Ritzy Chicken 65
Italian Chicken Spaghetti Casserole 66
No Tomato Chicken Spaghetti Casserole................... 67

"The finest gift a woman can give to her family, is the gift of a constructive and creative day."

POULTRY

1. **Time Required** for cooking poultry **Depends On the Size and Age** of the bird.

2. **Whole Birds** should be placed in a **Baking Dish** with or without roasting rack.

3. **Whole Birds** should be cooked on **70% Power 8-11 Minutes Per Pound.**

4. **Start Bird Breast Side Down,** turning half way through cooking time.

5. Brush with oleo or Micro-Shake browning seasoning or Kitchen Bouquet.

6. **May Cover with Wax Paper** to prevent splatter. **After Cooking Cover with Lid or Foil for Standing Time.**

7. **Standing Time is Important.** Let bird stand at least **10 Minutes** before serving.

8. You may use a microwave thermometer to test for doneness. Insert thermometer about 10 minutes before final cooking time. See chart for proper temperature.

9. Wrap foil around legs and wings half way through cooking time.

10. When baking cut-poultry, **Place Large and Meaty Portions on Outer Edge of Dish and Bony Parts in Center.**

11. **Rearrange cut-poultry Once** during cooking.

12. When cooking "Cooked Chicken" for use in casseroles or salads, always use water to keep from drying out. Cover tightly with glass lid or plastic wrap. Rearrange once during cooking. Use a 2-1/2 to 3 quart covered deep dish for one chicken. Store chicken broth for further use in soups, gumbos and sauces.

POULTRY DEFROSTING CHART
Power — Defrost or 30% Power

CUT	Defrosting Time Per Pound
Baked Whole Chicken	6 to 7 minutes
Chicken Parts	4 to 5 minutes
Turkcy, Whole - Breast, Bone In	5 to 7 minutes
Cornish Game Hen, Whole	6 to 8 minutes
Hens	7 to 8 minutes
Duck	8 to 9 minutes
Pheasant	8 to 9 minutes

POULTRY ROASTING CHART

CUT	POWER SETTING	COOKING TIME	Internal Temp. At End Of Cooking	Internal Temp. At End Of Standing Time
Baked Chicken, Whole	70% Power	8-11 min. per lb.	180-185°F	190-195°F
Chicken Parts	70% Power	8 min./lb.	180-185°F	190-195°F
Turkey, Whole	70% Power	10-12 min. per lb.	170-175°F	180-185°F
Turkey Breast (bone in)	70% Power	10-12 min. per lb.	170-175°F	180-185°F
Cornish Game Hen, Whole	70% Power	8 min./lb.	175-180°F	185-190°F
Hens	70% Power	12-15 min. per lb.	180-185°F	190-195°F
Duck	70% Power	7-10 min. per lb.	175-180°F	185-190°F
Pheasant	70% Power	9 min./lb.	175-180°F	185-190°F

NOTE: Chicken and cornish hens may also be cooked on **High** if desired.

ROAST CHICKEN

Utensils: 10″ browning skillet or dish with a roasting rack
inserted into dish
Time: 11 minutes per pound
Servings: 4

1 chicken (3 to 4 pounds)
oleo
salt
pepper

1.   Wash chicken. Season with salt and pepper. Rub with oleo. Place breast side down in browning skillet or dish with roasting rack. Roasting rack is not necessary. Micro on **70% Power for 11 Minutes Per Pound.** Half way during cooking time, turn chicken over and put foil around wing tips and lower half of legs. Do not cover while cooking. After cooking cover with lid or foil and let stand for 10-15 minutes.

NOTE: If desired, a probe or microwave cooking thermometer may be inserted halfway during cooking time. Insert into fleshy part of thigh or breast, away from bone. At end of cooking time, internal temperature should read 180-185 degrees. After standing, it should read 190-195 degrees.

NOTE: A microwave thermometer is a very good investment.

ROAST TURKEY

METHOD I:

COOKING TIME	Power Setting	Temp. At End Of Cooking	Temp. At End Of Standing Time
10-11 min. per pound	70% Power	170-175° F	180-185° F

METHOD II:

8-9 minutes per pound	HIGH first half of cooking time. 70% POWER second half of cooking time.	170-175° F	180-185° F

DIRECTIONS:

Completely thaw turkey. Wash and pat dry. Rub with salt, pepper, garlic and oleo. You may also rub with Kitchen Bouquet or other Micro Browning Seasoning available on market. Place turkey in 9" x 13" dish or any dish large enough. If you have an oven which has a turntable, you may use the turntable as a dish for turkey:

1. Place turkey BREAST SIDE DOWN on roasting rack (roasting rack optional). Cook 1/4 cooking time.

2. Turn turkey BREAST SIDE UP. Cook 1/4 more cooking time. Then if you are using Method II, you have to change your power setting from HIGH to 70% POWER for next cooking period (No. 3). Wrap turkey legs and wings with foil.

3. Return turkey back BREAST SIDE DOWN. Cook 1/4 more cooking time.

4. Return turkey back BREAST SIDE UP. At this point, insert probe or Microwave thermometer and cook last fourth of cooking time or when temperature reaches 170-175° F.

5. Cover with foil and let stand until temperature reaches 180-185° F. (About 15 minutes.)

NOTE: You can use turkeys which already have pop-up thermometers. They will pop up when done.

COOKED CHICKEN

Utensils: 3 quart deep dish and glass lid
Time: 25-30 minutes
Servings: 2-3 cups

1 chicken (2-3 pounds), cut or 6 to 8 meaty chicken parts depending on amount of meat called for in recipe
2 cups water, or more if more liquid is called for in recipe.

1. In 3 quart dish, put water and chicken. Cover with lid or plastic wrap. Micro on **High 25-30 Minutes,** or until tender. Drain and follow directions for recipe being used. Rearrange once during cooking so that any parts not covered by water will not dry out.

NOTE: Refrigerate all chicken stock for further use. Good for soups, gravies, gumbos and stews.

BARBECUED CHICKEN

Utensils: 4 quart Corning dish or casserole
Time: 30 minutes
Servings: 4-6

1 2 to 3 pound chicken, cut, or 2-3 pounds chicken parts

1. Wash chicken and put in 4 quart casserole.

1 cup onion, chopped
1-1/2 tablespoons mustard
1-1/2 teaspoons salt
3/4 teaspoon cayenne pepper
1/2 cup green onions, chopped
3 tablespoons brown sugar
1/3 cup cooking wine
1-1/2 tablespoons Worcester-shire sauce
2/3 cup celery, chopped
1/3 cup wine vinegar
2/3 cup tomato ketchup
1 chicken, cut

2. In 4 quart dish, put all ingredients. Micro on **High about 30 Minutes, Uncovered** until gravy is thick and chicken is tender. Rearrange once during cooking.

OVEN CRISPY CHICKEN

Utensils: Baking dish with ridges or use a
microwave roasting rack in dish
Time: 20-25 minutes
Servings: 4-6

**1 chicken (2-1/2 to 3 pounds)
cut or 4 chicken breasts
1/2 pint sour cream
1 teaspoon Italian
seasoning mix
1 cup crushed corn flake
crumbs**

1. Mix sour cream and Italian seasoning. Dip chicken in sour cream mixture, then in corn flakes. Place on baking dish, putting meatier parts around edge of dish and bony parts on inner part of dish. Micro on **High 20-25 Minutes, Covered** with wax paper. Turn pieces over half way during cooking time.

NOTE: In place of Italian seasoning mix, the following may be used: 1/2 teaspoon thyme, 2 teaspoons salt, 1/2 teaspoon oregano and a dash of garlic powder.

SWEET AND SOUR CHICKEN

Utensils: 7" x 11" oblong casserole dish
Time: 30 minutes
Servings: 6

**1 (2-1/2 to 3 pounds) chicken,
cut into pieces
salt & pepper to taste**

1. Season chicken with salt and pepper. Arrange in oblong casserole. Put meatier parts around outer edge of casserole and boney parts in center. Micro on **High 10 Minutes, Uncovered.**

**1 jar (8 oz.) Russian Salad
Dressing
1 jar (10 oz.) apricot preserves
1 envelope Lipton onion
soup mix
1-1/2 tablespoons cornstarch**

2. Turn chicken over. Mix together Russian Dressing, apricot preserves, onion soup mix and cornstarch. Pour over chicken. Micro on **High 20 Minutes.** Stir sauce around once or twice during cooking. **Cover** with wax paper to prevent splattering.

NOTE: Packaged chicken parts may be used instead of one cut chicken. If so, then cooking time should be added for any additional poundage.

CHICKEN ENCHILADA CASSEROLE

Utensils: 3 quart deep dish
7" x 11" oblong casserole dish
Time: 40 minutes
Servings: 6-8

**1 chicken, cut or
  2 cups cooked chicken
2 cups water**

1. In 3 quart dish, put chicken and water. Micro on **High 25 Minutes, Covered** with lid,, or until chicken is tender. Drain (reserve broth), cool and chop finely. Set aside.

**2 tablespoons oleo
1/3 cup onion, chopped**

2. In same 3 quart dish, put oleo and onion. Micro on **High 2 Minutes, Uncovered.**

**1 cup chicken broth
1 can (10 oz.) Ro-Tel tomatoes
  with chilies
1 package Taco Seasoning Mix**

3. Add chicken broth, tomatoes and Taco Mix. Micro on **High 5 Minutes.** Stir in chicken.

**1 package (12) corn tortillas
1-1/2 cups Cheddar or
  Monterey Jack cheese,
  grated
2 cups lettuce, shredded**

4. Pass each tortilla quickly through warm water. Layer 3 tortillas on bottom of 7" x 11" oblong casserole. Top with 1/3 red sauce. Next, top with 1/3 cheese. Next, top with 1/3 lettuce. Repeat with next 3 tortillas, etc. Micro on **High 8 Minutes, Uncovered.**

CHICKEN STEW

Utensils: 4 quart Corning dish
            4 cup glass measuring cup
Time: 57 minutes
Servings: 8

2/3 cup oil
2/3 cup flour

1. Roux: In 4 cup measuring cup, put oil and flour. Micro on **High 6-8 Minutes.** (See Roux). Stir just as Roux is turning color, then again every 30 seconds. Roux for chicken stew should be dark.

1 cup onion, chopped
1/2 cup celery, chopped
1/2 cup green onions, chopped
1/4 cup green pepper,
    chopped

2. Add onion, celery, green onions and green pepper. Micro on **High 5 Minutes.**

1 can (10-3/4 oz.) cream of
    chicken soup
1-3/4 cups hot water
1/4 cup parsley, chopped or
    1 tablespoon flakes
1 bay leaf
1 tablespoon salt
1/4 teaspoon black pepper
1/2 teaspoon cayenne pepper
— dash garlic powder
1 chicken (2-1/2 to 3 lbs.), cut

3   In 4 quart dish, put Roux. Stir in soup. Add water, parsley, bay leaf, salt, pepper, garlic powder and chicken. Micro on **High 25 Minutes, Covered** with lid; then Micro on **70% Power 10 Minutes, Covered.** Stir. Micro on **High 5 Minutes, Uncovered,** or until thick. Stir during cooking. Serve over rice.

CREAM OF CHICKEN QUICHE

Utensils: 3 quart dish
8″ or 9″ pie dish
Medium size mixing bowl
Time: 51 minutes
Servings: 8

1 chicken, cut or 6 meaty chicken parts
2 cups water
(See cooked chicken) or use step 1.

1. In 3 quart dish, put chicken and water. Micro on **High 25 Minutes, Covered** with lid, until tender. Drain, cool and debone. Chop fine. Set aside.

1 frozen pie shell, slightly defrosted

2. Put pie shell in glass pie dish. Micro on **High 4 Minutes.** Set aside.

3 slices bacon

3. In same 3 quart dish, put bacon. Micro on **High** about **3 Minutes,** until crisp. Remove from dripping. Reserve drippings.

1/4 cup onion, chopped
1/4 cup green onions, chopped
1/2 teaspoon salt
1/2 teaspoon pepper
cooked chicken

4. In 3 quart dish, add to bacon drippings: onion and green onions. Micro on **High 3 Minutes, Uncovered.** Add salt and pepper to onions. Mix in chicken. Set aside.

2 eggs, slightly beaten
1/3 cup milk
1/2 can (10 oz.) cream of chicken soup
1/2 cup Cheddar cheese, grated
salt and pepper to taste
crumbled bacon
3/4 cup Swiss cheese

5. In medium size mixing bowl, mix together: eggs, milk, cream of chicken soup, cheese, salt and pepper. Mix until thoroughly blended. Pour 1/3 mixture over pie crust. Top with chicken mixture. Sprinkle with crumbled bacon. Sprinkle with Swiss cheese. Pour remaining egg mixture over cheese. Micro on **70% Power 14-16 Minutes, Covered** with round glass lid or plastic wrap. Micro until set. Let stand 10 minutes.

NOTE: In Step 1, rearrange chicken once during cooking.

NOTE: For regular quiche, omit chicken and Step 1.

GOLDEN CHICKEN OR TURKEY SOUFFLE

Utensils: 7" x 11" oblong casserole dish
            2 quart dish
Time: 23 minutes
Servings: 6-8

2 to 3 cups diced cooked chicken or turkey (see cooked chicken) Reserve broth.

1.   See COOKED CHICKEN.

2 cups chicken broth (if no reserved broth, use canned chicken broth)
1 tablespoon onion, chopped
1/3 cup celery, chopped

2.   In 2 quart dish, put chicken broth, onion and celery. Micro on **High 5 Minutes.**

1-1/2 cups plain bread crumbs
4 eggs, slightly beaten
2 teaspoons poultry seasoning, (optional)
1/4 teaspoon salt

3.   In 7" x 11" oblong casserole, put chicken, chicken broth mixture, bread crumbs, eggs, poultry seasoning and salt. Mix thoroughly. Micro on **70% Power 12 Minutes.** Let stand 10 minutes. Pour on topping. Serve hot.

1 can (10-3/4 oz.) cream of mushroom soup
1/4 cup milk
1 cup American cheese, grated or 1 cup Cheez Whiz (processed cheese spread)

4.   In 2 quart dish, put soup, milk and cheese. Micro on **High 6 Minutes** until cheese is melted and hot. Serve over souffle.

HERBED CHICKEN

Utensils: Flat casserole dish (put a microwave roasting rack in dish)
Time: 30 minutes
Servings: 6

1 chicken cut or 2-3 packages chicken parts
1 cup unseasoned bread crumbs
1/2 cup Parmesan cheese
1/4 cup thyme
2 teaspoons basil
2 teaspoons salt
1/2 teaspoon cayenne pepper

1. Mix together bread crumbs, cheese, thyme, basil, salt and pepper. Set aside.

8 tablespoons oleo, melted

2. Dip chicken in oleo, then roll in crumb mixture. Place in casserole dish on roasting rack. Place meat or parts around outer part of dish and bony parts in center of dish. Micro on **High 20-30 Minutes, Uncovered,** or until chicken is completely tender. During half-way of cooking, turn over and rearrange chicken. Let stand 15 minutes.

NOTE: Italian bread crumbs may be used in place of unseasoned crumbs. If so, omit thyme and basil.

NOTE: For variation: 1 jar (15-1/2 oz.) Ragu spaghetti sauce may be poured over chicken last 15 minutes of cooking.

HOT CHICKEN SALAD CASSEROLE

Utensils: 2-1/2 - 3 quart dish
4 cup glass measuring cup
8" x 8" square dish or similar
Time: 13 minutes
Servings: 8

1 chicken (2-3 pounds), cut

1. See cooked chicken. Drain chicken. Debone and chop in chunks. May use food processor if chicken is desired chopped finer. Set chicken aside.

3 tablespoons oleo
2/3 cup celery, chopped
1/2 cup onion, chopped

2. In 4 cup measure, put oleo, celery and onion. Micro on **High 5 Minutes.** If celery is put in food processor do not saute' in oleo, leave raw. Saute' only onion.

2 cups chicken, cooked
    and chopped
1/2 cup mayonnaise
1 can (10-3/4 oz.) cream of
    chicken soup
1/2 teaspoon pepper
1/4 teaspoon salt
3 hard boiled eggs, chopped
juice of one lemon
    (2 tablespoons)
1/2 cup almonds (optional)

3. In 8" x 8" square (or similar) dish, mix onion and celery, chicken, mayonnaise, soup, pepper, salt, eggs, lemon juice and almonds. Micro on **High 8 Minutes, Uncovered.**

1-1/2 to 2 cups crushed
    potato chips

4. Mix in potato chips or sprinkle on top. Serve hot.

63

MANDARIN CHICKEN

Utensils: 4 quart Corning dish
Time: 32 minutes
Servings: 6

**1 chicken (2-1/2 to 3 pounds)
      cut, or 4 to 6 breasts cut
      in half
salt and pepper to taste
4 tablespoons oleo or butter**

1.   Season chicken with salt and pepper. On top of range in 4 quart Corning dish, heat butter. Add chicken and brown slightly.

1/4 cup onion, chopped

2.   Add onion and Micro on **High 2 Minutes.**

**1-1/2 tablespoons cornstarch
1/2 teaspoon ginger
2 tablespoons brown sugar
1 can (11 oz.) Mandarin
      orange segments,
      drained. (Reserve juice)
2 tablespoons soy sauce
1 can chicken broth
      (1 cup)**

3.   In small bowl, mix together, cornstarch, ginger, sugar, Mandarin orange juice, soy sauce and chicken broth. Pour over chicken and Micro on **High 20 Minutes, Covered.** Add Mandarin orange slices and Micro on **High 10 Minutes, Uncovered.** Rearrange chicken once during cooking.

RITZY CHICKEN

Utensils: 3 quart deep dish
7" x 11" oblong casserole dish
Medium dish
Time: 42 minutes
Servings: 8

1 chicken (2-1/2 to 3 pounds), cut
1-1/2 cups water

1. In 3 quart dish, put chicken and water. Cover with lid. Micro on **High 25 Minutes,** or until tender. Remove chicken. Reserve 1 cup chicken stock. Debone chicken. Chop into chunks. Set aside.

8 tablespoons oleo
1 box (8 oz.) Ritz Crackers, crushed

2. In 7" x 11" oblong dish, melt oleo. Add crackers. Mix together. Press to form a crust.

1 cup onion, chopped
1/2 cup celery, chopped
3 tablespoons oil

3. In medium dish, put onion, celery and oil. Micro on **High 9 Minutes.**

1 can (10-3/4 oz.) cream of mushroom soup
1 carton (8 oz.) sour cream
1 cup chicken stock
1/4 teaspoon garlic powder
salt and pepper to taste

4. Add soup, sour cream, chicken stock, garlic powder, salt and pepper, and chopped chicken. Pour over Ritz cracker crust. Micro on **High 8 Minutes, Uncovered.**

ITALIAN CHICKEN SPAGHETTI CASSEROLE

Utensils: 3 quart casserole round dish
4 quart Corning casserole dish or
(7" x 11" oblong casserole may be used)
Time: 53 minutes
Servings: 6-8

1 chicken (2-1/2 to 3 pounds) cut or 6-8 meaty parts
2 cups hot water
1 cup onion, chopped
2/3 cup celery, chopped
1 cup green pepper, chopped
1/4 teaspoon parsley flakes or 1 teaspoon fresh parsley, chopped

1. In 3 quart round dish, put chicken, water, onion, celery, green pepper and parsley. Micro on **High 30 Minutes, Covered,** stirring occasionally. Remove chicken from broth. Debone and chop in chunks.

2 cans (10 oz.) tomatoes, mashed
1 small jar pimentos, drained and chopped (optional)
1 can (4 oz.) mushrooms, drained
1 can (6 oz.) tomato paste
1 small jar (3 oz.) olives, drained and chopped
2 teaspoons salt
1/2 plus 1/4 teaspoon cayenne pepper
1/4 teaspoon black pepper
1/4 teaspoon garlic powder
1/4 teaspoon basil
1-1/4 cups boiling water
1 package (12 oz.) thin spaghetti

2. Add tomatoes, pimientos, mushrooms, tomato paste, olives, salt, pepper, garlic powder, basil, water and spaghetti (broken in small pieces.) Micro on **High 15-20 Minutes, Uncovered,** or until tender, stirring once or twice.

2 cups Cheddar cheese, grated

3. In 4 quart casserole (or 7" x 11" oblong casserole), put a layer of chicken, then a layer of spaghetti, then a layer of cheese. Repeat chicken, spaghetti and cheese. Micro on **High 8 Minutes, Covered** with wax paper. (Wax paper prevents splatter.)

NOTE: Remove excess skin on some chicken parts for Step 1.

NO TOMATO CHICKEN SPAGHETTI CASSEROLE

Utensils: 3 quart deep dish
7" x 11" flat casserole dish or 4 quart Corning dish
Time: 53 minutes
Servings: 6-8

1 chicken (2-1/2 to 3 pounds), cut
2 cups hot water
2 cups onion, chopped
1 cup celery, chopped
1 cup green pepper, chopped
1-1/4 teaspoons cayenne pepper
1/4 teaspoon black pepper
2-1/2 teaspoons salt
1/2 teaspoon poultry seasoning
1/4 teaspoon garlic powder
1 teaspoon parsley flakes
1/4 teaspoon Worcestershire sauce

1. In 3 quart dish, put chicken, water, onion, celery, green pepper, cayenne and black pepper, salt, poultry seasoning, garlic powder, parsley flakes and Worcestershire sauce. Micro on **High 30 Minutes, Covered.** Remove chicken from broth. Debone and chop in chunks. Set chicken aside. (Rearrange chicken once during cooking.)

1 jar (3 oz.) olives, drained and chopped
1 can (4 oz.) mushrooms, drained
1/4 teaspoon (any type) cooking wine (optional)
1 package (12 oz.) thin spaghetti
2-1/2 cups boiling water
2 tablespoons oleo

2. To broth add olives, mushrooms, wine, spaghetti (broken in pieces), hot water and oleo. Micro on **High 15-20 Minutes, Uncovered,** or until tender. Put in a 7" x 11" oblong casserole or a 4 quart dish.

1/3 cup Parmesan cheese
1 cup Cheddar cheese, grated
1/3 cup Italian bread crumbs

3. Mix in Parmesan cheese and chicken. Sprinkle with Cheddar cheese, then with bread crumbs. Micro on **High 8 Minutes, Covered** with wax paper to prevent splatter.

Seafood

SEAFOOD
Hints on Seafood 70
Defrosting Seafood 70
Seafood Cooking Chart 70

FISH
Baked Flounder with Crab Stuffing 71
Catfish or Trout Broiled in Butter Sauce 72
Red Fish or Trout Alexandra 73

SHRIMP
Barbecued Shrimp 74
Barbecued Shrimp La Sal and Sams 74
Italian Steamed Shrimp 75
Shrimp and Crab Stew 76
Shrimp Creole 77
Shrimp in Crabmeat Sauce 78
Shrimp Scampi 79

CRABS
Baked Crabmeat Casserole 80
Crabmeat Artichoke Au Gratin 81
Crabmeat Au Gratin 82
Prize Winning Crabmeat Patties 83

CRAWFISH
Crawfish Delicacy 84
Crawfish Etouffee 85
Crawfish Rice Casserole 86

OYSTERS
Oysters Bienville or Casserole 87
Oysters Broussard 88
Oysters Conrad 89
Herbed Oysters 90

Tuna Mushroom Bake 91

Salmon in Tomato Sauce 92

Seafood Bake 93

FISH AND SEAFOOD

1. In cooking fish and seafood, the number one rule is to **Avoid Overcooking.**

2. Fish and seafood are high in moisture content; therefore, **Requires a Very Short Cooking Time.**

3   Cooking time for fish and seafood is generally **4-6 Minutes Per Pound.**

4. Fish and seafood **Should Be Covered** with lid or plastic wrap for faster cooking and to retain moisture.

5. Whole fish **Should Be Turned Once** during cooking.

6. When fish is cooked it can be **Easily Flaked with a Fork.**

7. Shellfish is cooked when the **Meat Appears Opaque** and the **Shell Turns Pink.**

8. When arranging fish in a dish or casserole, **Place The Thickest Part** of steaks or fillets at **Outer Edges of Container.** Overlap the thin edges of fillets for more uniform cooking.

SEAFOOD DEFROSTING CHART
Power — 30%

SEAFOOD	Defrosting Time Per Pound
Fish Fillets	10 - 12 min.
Fish Steaks	6 - 7 min.
Whole Fish 1½ - 2 lbs.	13 - 14 min.
Shrimp	5 - 6 min.
Crabmeat	15 min.

NOTE: Standing time is the same as defrosting time.

COOKING SEAFOOD

Seafood	Time	Power	Standing Time
Fish Fillets			
1 lb.	4 - 6 min.	High	4 - 5 min.
2 lb.	8 - 9 min.	High	4 - 5 min.
Fish Steaks	5 - 6 min./lb.	High	5 - 6 min.
Whole Fish 1½ - 2 lbs.	10 - 13 min. Complete Time	High	4 - 5 min.
Shrimp	5 - 7 min./lb.	70% Power	4 min.

70

BAKED FLOUNDER WITH CRAB STUFFING

Utensils: 7" x 11" oblong casserole dish
           1-1/2 quart dish
Time: 19 minutes
Servings: 4

2 one pound flounders
salt and pepper to taste

1. Wash and dry fish. Season with salt and pepper. Slit a large pocket in each fish. (You may want to ask your butcher to do so for you.)

2 tablespoons oleo
1 cup onion, chopped

2. In 1-1/2 quart dish, put oleo and onion. Micro on **High 3 Minutes.**

2 tablespoons green onions,
        chopped
2 cloves garlic, minced
1/4 cup celery, chopped
1/4 cup green bell pepper,
        chopped
1 tablespoon parsley, chopped

3. Add green onions, garlic, celery, bell pepper and parsley. Micro on **High 3 Minutes.**

1 cup frozen white crabmeat,
        defrosted (1/2 pound)

4. Add crabmeat. Micro on **High 3 Minutes.**

3/4 cup bread crumbs
1 tablespoon salt
1/8 teaspoon black pepper
1/8 teaspoon thyme
1 egg, beaten
6 tablespoons oleo, melted

5. Mix in bread crumbs, salt, pepper, thyme and egg. Stuff into flounders. Place in oblong casserole dish. Drizzle with oleo. **Cover** with plastic wrap. Micro on **High 10-12 Minutes.** Turn fish over half way of cooking time. Fish is cooked when fish flakes easily with a fork.

CATFISH OR TROUT
BROILED IN BUTTER SAUCE

Utensils: 7" x 11" oblong casserole dish or other flat dish
Time: 11 minutes
Servings: 4

**1/2 to 1 pound trout or
    catfish fillets
1/4 cup butter (not oleo)
1/2 cup onion, chopped
2 tablespoons green onions,
    chopped**

1. In casserole dish, put butter, onion and green onions. Micro on **High 3 Minutes, Uncovered.**

**2 tablespoons lemon juice
2 tablespoons fresh parsley
    chopped or 1 tablespoon
    parsley flakes
salt and pepper to taste
1/4 teaspoon cooking wine
2 drops Worcestershire sauce**

2. Season fish with salt and pepper. Put fish in casserole. Do not overlap. Add lemon juice, parlsey, salt, pepper, wine and Worcestershire sauce. Micro on **High 5 Minutes, Covered** with plastic wrap. Micro on **70% Power, 2-3 Minutes, Covered** with plastic wrap. Let stand 5 minutes. Fish is done when it can be flaked with a fork.

NOTE: Cook all fish 4-6 minutes per pound.

RED FISH OR TROUT ALEXANDRA
(With Shrimp and Oyster Sauce)

Utensils: 7″ x 11″ oblong casserole
Small bowl
Time: 21 minutes
Servings: 6

5 medium trout or
   1 (3 pound) trout or
   2-1/2 to 3 pound redfish
2 tablespoons lemon juice
1/2 cup oleo, melted
salt and pepper to taste

1. Season fish with salt and pepper. Place fish in oblong dish. Pour lemon juice and oleo over fish. Cover with plastic wrap. Micro on **High 6 Minutes.** Turn fish over. Micro on **High 6** more **Minutes, Covered** with plastic wrap. Fish is done when it can be flaked easily with a fork.

SAUCE:

6 tablespoons oleo
1 to 1-1/2 dozens oysters or
   1 pint, drained well
   (reserve juice)
2 tablespoons parsley,
   chopped
1/4 cup green onions, chopped

2. In small bowl, put oleo, oysters, parsley and green onions. Micro on **High 5 Minutes.**

2 tablespoons flour
— dash garlic powder
salt and pepper to taste
1/4 cup milk
1 tablespoon cooking wine
1 to 1-1/2 pounds shrimp,
   boiled, peeled and
   chopped
oyster liquid

3. Stir in flour. Add garlic powder, salt and pepper, milk, cooking wine, shrimp and oyster liquid. Micro on **High 3 Minutes,** stirring once or twice. Pour over fish. Cover with plastic wrap. Micro on **High 1 Minute.** Let stand 5 minutes.

NOTE: Any type fish or fish fillets may be used in place of trout or red fish.

NOTE: Fish should be cooked about 4 minutes per pound.

BARBECUED SHRIMP

Utensils: 10" browning skillet or 2-1/2 to 3 quart Corning dish
Time: 25 minutes
Servings: 4

1 cup onion, chopped
1 tablespoon mustard
1 teaspoon salt
1/2 teaspoon cayenne pepper
1/3 cup green onions, chopped
2 tablespoons brown sugar
1/4 cup cooking wine
1 tablespoon Worcestershire
**   sauce**
1/3 cup celery, chopped
1/8 cup wine vinegar
1/2 cup tomato ketchup

1. In 10" browning skillet or Corning dish, mix all ingredients except shrimp. Micro on **High 15 Minutes, Covered** with wax paper. Stir during cooking.

1-1/2 to 2 pounds raw shrimp, peeled

2. Add shrimp and Micro on **High 10 Minutes, Covered** with lid. Stir during cooking.

BARBECUED SHRIMP LA SAL AND SAMS

Utensils: 10" browning skillet or 7" x 11" oblong casserole dish
Time: 10 minutes
Servings: 4-6

2-1/2 to 3 pounds large shrimp,
**   peeled or unpeeled**
1 block oleo, melted
1-1/2 tablespoons salt
2 tablespoons black pepper
1 teaspoon thyme
1/2 cup barbecue sauce
1 tablespoon lemon juice
Italian bread crumbs

1. In skillet or oblong dish, put shrimp, oleo, salt, pepper, thyme and barbecue sauce. Micro on **High 10 Minutes, Covered** with lid or plastic wrap. Sprinkle with 1/3 cup bread crumbs. Micro on **High 5 Minutes, Covered** with lid or plastic wrap. Let stand 7-10 minutes. Stir once during cooking.

ITALIAN STEAMED SHRIMP

Utensils: 10" browning skillet or 7" x 11" oblong casserole dish
Time: 15 minutes
Servings: 4-6

1/2 cup olive oil
1/4 cup wine vinegar
1 cup onion, chopped
1/2 cup green onions, chopped
1/2 cup celery, chopped
juice of 2 lemons or
    4 tablespoons lemon juice
2 tablespoons salt
1/2 tablespoon cayenne
    pepper
1 tablespoon black pepper
1/2 teaspoon Italian seasoning

1. In skillet or oblong dish, put all ingredients except shrimp. Micro on **High 5 Minutes, Uncovered.**

2-1/2 to 3 pounds large shrimp, unpeeled

2. Add shrimp, Micro on **High 10-12 Minutes, Covered** with lid or plastic wrap. When shrimp turn pink they are done. Let stand 7-10 minutes. Stir during cooking.

SHRIMP AND CRAB STEW

Utensils: 4 cup glass measuring cup
3 quart deep dish casserole
Time: 41-46 minutes
Servings: 6

2/3 cup flour
2/3 cup oil

1. Roux: In 4 cup measuring cup, put flour and oil. Micro on **High 7-9 Minutes,** or until golden brown. Stir at about 6-1/2 minutes, just as Roux starts to darken (or Roux may burn).

2/3 cup onion, chopped

2. Add onion. Micro on **High 3 Minutes.**

1/4 cup green pepper, chopped
1/3 cup green onions, chopped
1/4 cup celery, chopped
(optional)

3. Add green peppers, green onions and celery. Micro on **High 2-3 Minutes,** stirring, until sauteed.

1 package frozen crabs
6-12 crab pieces
1/4 cup parsley, chopped or
1 tablespoon parsley
flakes
1 bay leaf
1/2 teaspoon cayenne pepper
1/4 teaspoon black pepper
1-1/2 teaspoons salt
1/4 teaspoon garlic powder
2-1/2 cups HOT water

4. Put roux mixture in 3 quart dish. Add crabs, parsley, bay leaf, pepper, salt, garlic powder and hot water. Micro on **High 10 Minutes, Uncovered.**

1-1/2 to 2 pounds raw shrimp,
peeled
1 small can (5-3/4 oz.) mush-
room steak sauce

5. Add shrimp and steak sauce. Micro on **70% Power** for **20-25 Minutes** or until thick.

SHRIMP CREOLE

Utensils: 2-1/2 quart dish
Time: 37 minutes
Servings: 6

1/3 cup oil
1/3 cup flour

1. Roux: (See roux.) In 2-1/2 quart dish, put oil and flour. Micro on **High 6-7 Minutes.** Stir just as roux begins to change color (or roux may burn). As roux darkens, stir again.

1 cup onion, chopped
2/3 cup green onions, chopped
1/2 cup celery, chopped
1/2 cup green pepper, chopped

2. Add onion, green onions, celery and green pepper. Micro on **High 6 Minutes,** or until sauteed. Stir at least once.

1 teaspoon salt
1/4 teaspoon pepper
1 can (8 oz.) tomato sauce
1 cup tomato ketchup
1-1/2 cups water
1 bay leaf
1/4 teaspoon sweet basil

3. Add salt, pepper, tomato sauce, tomato ketchup, water, bay leaf and basil. Micro on **High 10 Minutes, Covered.** Stir once or twice during cooking.

1-1/2 to 2 pounds raw shrimp, peeled and deveined

4. Add shrimp. Micro on **70% Power 15 Minutes, Covered.** Stir once or twice during cooking. More salt or pepper may be added if desired.

SHRIMP IN CRABMEAT SAUCE

Utensils: 3 quart dish
            2-1/2 quart dish
Time: 25 minutes
Servings: 6-8

6 tablespoons oleo
1 carton (8 oz.) fresh mush-
**   rooms, washed and sliced**

1. In 3 quart dish, put oleo and mushrooms. Micro on **High** about **7 Minutes, Covered** until tender. Set aside.

8 tablespoons oleo
2 cups onion, chopped
5 cloves garlic, minced

2. In 1-1/2 quart dish, put oleo, onion and garlic. Micro on **High 6- 8 Minutes.** Add mushrooms in 3 quart dish.

2 tablespoons cornstarch
1 cup water
1/4 cup soy sauce
1/2 cup white cooking wine
1 pound white lump crabmeat,
**   defrosted**
2 pounds shrimp, boiled and
**   peeled**
Hot pepper sauce to taste
salt and pepper to taste

3. Stir in cornstarch. Slowly stir in water, soy sauce, wine, crabmeat, shrimp, hot sauce, salt, pepper and mushrooms and their juices. Micro on **70% Power 12-15 Minutes,** until mixture thickens. Let stand 10 minutes. You may transfer to a flat casserole dish in step 3.

SHRIMP SCAMPI

Utensils: 10" browning skillet or similar Corning or flat dish
Time: about 10 minutes
Servings: 6-8

**1-1/2 to 2 pounds raw shrimp,
  peeled**
**1 block butter or oleo,
  (8 tablespoons)**
**2 cloves garlic, peeled
  and whole**

1. In 10" skillet or similar dish, put shrimp, butter and garlic cloves. Micro on **High** until all shrimp turn pink, **Covered.** Stir once or twice.

2 tablespoons flour
1/4 teaspoon cayenne pepper
1/4 teaspoon black pepper
1/2 teaspoon salt
juice of 1 lemon (2 tablespoons)
1/2 cup water
1/4 teaspoon parsley flakes

2. Stir in flour. Add pepper, salt and lemon juice. Stir in water slowly. Add parsley flakes. Micro on **High** until sauce is thick, stirring occasionally, **Uncovered.** Serve hot. Dunk garlic bread in sauce.

NOTE: More water may be added if sauce is too thick.

BAKED CRABMEAT CASSEROLE

Utensils: 2 quart casserole dish
　　　　　　8″ x 8″ square dish
Time: 15 minutes
Servings: 6

6 tablespoons oleo
1 cup onion, chopped
1/2 cup green pepper, chopped
1/2 cup green onions, chopped
1/2 cup celery, chopped

1 pound white lump crabmeat, defrosted
1 cup mayonnaise
3 tablespoons Worcestershire sauce
1 tablespoon Tabasco sauce
4 tablespoons lemon juice
1 cup bread crumbs

1. In 2 quart dish, put oleo, onion, green pepper, green onions and celery. Micro on **High 7-8 Minutes,** until completely sauteed.

2. Stir in crabmeat, mayonnaise, Worcestershire sauce, Tabasco sauce and lemon juice. Mix well. Put in square dish. Top with bread crumbs. Micro on **High 8 Minutes.**

NOTE: Shrimp (1 pound, boiled and peeled) may be added to this casserole.

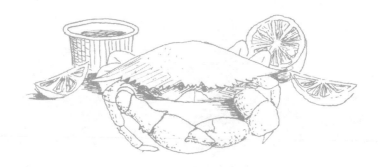

CRABMEAT ARTICHOKE AU GRATIN

Utensils: 10" browning skillet or 7" x 11" oblong casserole
Time: 10 minutes
Servings: 6

**1 pound white lump crab meat,
    thawed**
**2 cans cream of mushroom
    soup**
salt and pepper to taste
— dash garlic powder
— dash celery salt or
1/4 cup celery, chopped finely
1 teaspoon parsley flakes or
  **2 tablespoons fresh parsley,
    chopped**
2 tablespoons lemon juice
**1 large can (8-1/2 oz.)
    artichokes, drained and
    chopped large**

1. In casserole or skillet mix all
   ingredients.

1 cup American cheese, grated
1/4 cup Italian bread crumbs

2. Top with cheese and bread
   crumbs. Micro on **High 10
   Minutes.**

CRABMEAT AU GRATIN

Utensils: 3 quart dish or 8 cup batter bowl
Sea shells, ramekins or Au Gratin dishes
Time: 11 minutes
Servings: 8

1 cup onion, chopped
1/4 cup celery, chopped fine
8 tablespoons oleo or butter
(1 block)

1. In 3 quart dish, put oleo, onion and celery. Micro on **High 4 Minutes.**

1/3 cup flour
2 small cans (5.33 oz.)
evaporated milk

2. Stir in flour. Add milk gradually.

2 egg yolks
1 teaspoon salt
1/2 teaspoon cayenne pepper
1/4 teaspoon black pepper
1/4 teaspoon garlic powder

3. Stir in egg yolks, salt, pepper and garlic powder. Micro on **High 2-3 Minutes, Uncovered,** until very thick. Stir once or twice during cooking.

1 pound claw crabmeat
(see note)
1 jar (8 oz.) Cheez Whiz
1/4 cup Italian bread crumbs
Cheddar cheese

4. Stir in crabmeat, Cheez Whiz and bread crumbs. Micro on **High 4 Minutes.** Spoon in sea shells or Au Gratin dishes. Sprinkle with Cheddar cheese. Micro on **High** until cheese melts.

NOTE: If no sea shells available put crabmeat into flat casserole dish and serve as a casserole.

NOTE: White crabmeat may be substituted for claw crabmeat.

PRIZE WINNING CRABMEAT PATTIES

Utensils: 2 quart dish
           2 quart dish
           Patty shells or shallow casserole dish
Time: 18 minutes
Servings: 50

50 miniature patty shells

1. Bake patty shells and set aside.

2 tablespoons oleo
1/2 cup green onions,
    finely chopped
1/4 cup green pepper,
    finely chopped
1 tablespoon celery leaves,
    finely chopped

2. In 2 quart dish, put oleo, green onions green pepper and celery leaves. Micro on **High 5 Minutes.**

1/4 teaspoon garlic puree
1 pound lump crabmeat, thawed
1 cup Italian bread crumbs
1/8 teaspoon cayenne pepper
1/8 teaspoon grated lemon peel
    or 1 teaspoon lemon juice
1/4 teaspoon salt

3. Add garlic and crabmeat. Micro on **High 4 Minutes.** Stir in bread crumbs, pepper, lemon peel and salt. Mix well and set aside. Mixture will be dry.

SAUCE:

2 tablespoons oleo
1/2 tablespoon green onions,
    chopped finely

4. In 2 quart dish, put oleo and green onions. Micro on **High 1 Minute.**

1 tablespoon flour
1 cup milk
1/2 cup Cheddar cheese,
    grated
1/4 cup Monterey Jack cheese,
    grated
1 tablespoon Parmesan cheese
1/2 tablespoon lemon juice
2 dashes Tabasco sauce
1/4 teaspoon dry mustard

5. Stir in flour. Slowly stir in milk, then cheeses, lemon juice, Tabasco sauce and mustard. Micro on **50% Power 5-7 Minutes.** Sauce should be rather thin. Pour sauce over crabmeat mixture. Blend, but do not mix thoroughly. Stuff patty shells or put in shallow casserole dish. Micro on **70% Power 3 Minutes** or until hot. Serve hot.

CRAWFISH DELICACY

Utensils: 3 quart deep dish
Time: 42 minutes
Servings: 6

1/2 cup oil
1 cup onion, chopped
1/4 cup green pepper,
  chopped
1/4 cup celery, chopped

1. In 3 quart dish, put oil, onion, green pepper and celery. Micro on **High 6-8 Minutes,** until saute'ed.

1-1/2 to 2 pounds peeled
  crawfish tails

2. Add crawfish tails. Micro on **High 6 Minutes.**

3 tablespoons flour
1 package McCormick's Beef
  Stew Seasoning Mix
1/2 cup green onions, chopped
1/4 cup parsley, chopped
1 teaspoon salt
1/2 teaspoon cayenne pepper
1/4 teaspoon black pepper
— dash garlic powder
3 cups hot water

3. Stir in flour, Beef Stew Mix, green onions, parsley, salt, pepper, garlic powder and water. Micro on **High 15 Minutes, Uncovered,** stirring once or twice. Then Micro on **50% Power 15 Minutes, Covered.** Stir once or twice during cooking.

NOTE: If gravy is too thick, add a little water. If gravy is too thin, cook a little longer, uncovered.

CRAWFISH ETOUFFEE

Utensils: 2-1/2 quart deep dish casserole
Time: 27 minutes
Servings: 6-8

1 stick oleo or (8 tablespoons)
1 cup onion, chopped
2/3 cup green pepper,
chopped
1/2 cup celery, chopped

1. In 2-1/2 quart deep dish, put oleo, onion, green pepper and celery. Micro on **High 10-12 Minutes,** or until tender.

1 to 1-1/2 pounds crawfish tails,
peeled (about 3 cups)
1/4 cup green onions, chopped

2. Add crawfish tails and green onions. Micro on **High 5 Minutes, Covered** with lid.

2 tablespoons flour
1/4 cup parsley, chopped or
1 tablespoon parsley
flakes
2 teaspoons tomato paste
1 cup Hot water
salt and pepper to taste
— dash garlic powder

3. Stir in flour. Add parsley, tomato paste, water, salt, pepper and garlic powder. Micro on **70% Power 10 Minutes, Uncovered,** until thick. Stir once or twice during cooking.

CRAWFISH RICE CASSEROLE
(Similar to a Crawfish Jambalaya)

Utensils: 3 quart casserole
4 cup glass measuring cup
Time: 38 minutes
Servings: 6-8

1/2 cup oleo (8 tablespoons)
1 to 1-1/2 pounds crawfish tails
1/4 teaspoon cayenne pepper
1/4 teaspoon salt
— dash garlic powder

1. In 3 quart dish, put oleo. Micro on **High 3 Minutes.** Add crawfish, salt, pepper and garlic powder.

1 small can (4 oz.) mushrooms,
     drained, reserve liquid
2 cans (10 oz.) onion soup
water plus other liquids
     to make 4 cups

2. Add mushrooms to crawfish. In 4 cup measuring cup, put mushroom liquid, soup and enough water to make 4 cups liquid. Add to crawfish. Micro on **High 5 Minutes,** until boiling.

2 cups rice, uncooked

3. Add rice. Micro on **50% Power** for **30 Minutes, Covered.** (Stir after 15 minutes of cooking.) Let stand 10 minutes.

OYSTERS BIENVILLE OR CASSEROLE

Utensils: 10″ Corning Browning Skillet
Oyster shells or ramekins
Time: 17-29 minutes
Servings: 4

3 tablespoons butter

1. In browning dish, heat butter on **High 2 Minutes.**

1 pint oysters (15-20), drained and dried with paper towels
1 pound raw shrimp, peeled and chopped small

2. Add shrimp and oysters. Micro on **High 3 Minutes, Uncovered.** Remove oysters and set aside.

1/4 teaspoon garlic powder
1/4 teaspoon salt
1/4 teaspoon cayenne pepper
2 tablespoons green onions, chopped
1/2 teaspoon Worcestershire sauce

3. To shrimp add garlic powder, salt, pepper, green onions and Worcestershire sauce. Micro on **High 3 Minutes, Uncovered.**

1/4 cup flour
1/2 cup evaporated milk
1 tablespoon wine
1 teaspoon parsley flakes or fresh parsley
1 can (4 oz.) mushrooms, chopped and drained, reserve juice
1 cup oyster juice, (see note)
Italian bread crumbs
Parmesan cheese

4. Stir in slowly: flour, cream, wine, parsley, mushrooms and oyster juice. Micro on **High 5 Minutes** or until mixture thickens, stirring to prevent lumping. Put 1 or 2 oysters on each shell. Spoon sauce over oysters. Cover heavily with bread crumbs, then heavily with cheese. Place 5 shells on dish. Place in oven and Micro on **High 4 Minutes.** Repeat with next 5 shells. Serve hot.

NOTE: If casserole is desired, add oysters to sauce in browning dish. Top with bread crumbs, then cheese. Micro on **High 8 Minutes.** (Step 4)

NOTE: If oyster juice does not amount to 1 cup, add reserved mushroom juice to equal 1 cup.

SEAFOOD

OYSTERS BROUSSARD
(Oysters topped with Crabmeat and Artichokes)

Utensils: 3 quart dish
Oyster shells or ramekins
2 quart dish
Time: 25 minutes
Servings: 6

6 tablespoons oleo
1/2 cup green onions, chopped
1/4 cup celery, chopped
1/4 cup parsley, chopped

1. In 3 quart dish, put oleo, onions, celery and parsley. Micro on **High 3 Minutes.**

1/2 pound fresh mushrooms, washed, drained and chopped fine

2. Add mushrooms. Micro on **High 5 Minutes.**

1 can (10 oz.) tomatoes, drained and mashed
2 cans (8 oz.) artichokes, drained and pureed

3. Add tomatoes and artichokes. Micro on **High 5 Minutes.** Stir once or twice during cooking.

1 cup whipping cream
1/2 pound crabmeat, defrosted
1/4 teaspoon garlic powder
salt and pepper to taste
1/4 cup cooking sherry
1/2 cup bread crumbs

4. Add whipping cream, crabmeat, garlic powder, salt, pepper and sherry. Micro on **High 5 Minutes.** Stir once or twice during cooking. Stir in bread crumbs. If sauce is too thin add more bread crumbs.

3 dozen oysters and liquid (about 1 pint)

5. In 2 quart dish, put oysters and liquid. Micro on **High 5 Minutes,** until oysters curl. Put 2 or 3 oysters in each shell. Put a little oyster liquid over each oyster. Top with crabmeat mixture.

1 cup Parmesan cheese, grated

6. Sprinkle each with Parmesan cheese. Micro on **High** about **2 Minutes,** until cheese melts.

OYSTERS CONRAD
(Oysters in Garlic Sauce)

Utensils: 2 quart dish
Oyster shells or ramekins
Bacon rack or plate lined with paper towels
Time: 15-17 minutes
Servings: 4-6

1/2 pound bacon

1. Place bacon on bacon rack in strips. Micro on **High** about **45 Seconds** per slice or until crisp. Remove bacon and crumble. Set aside.

2 sticks oleo or butter
5 cloves garlic, crushed
1 pint oysters (and liquid)
   about 2-1/2 to 3 dozen
   oysters
1 tablespoon flour
parsley flakes
Italian seasoning
Tabasco sauce

2. In 2 quart dish, put oleo. Micro on **High** until melted. Add garlic, oyster juice and oysters. Micro on **High 4 Minutes.** Remove oysters. Set aside. Stir flour into oyster juice. Micro on **High** about **2-3 Minutes,** until slightly thick. Put about 3 oysters on each shell. Sprinkle with bacon. Pour sauce over bacon. Sprinkle with parsley, then with Italian seasoning, then with a few drops of Tabasco sauce. Micro on **High 3 Minutes,** until hot and bubbly.

HERBED OYSTERS

Utensils: 2 quart shallow dish
                Shells or ramekins
Time: 10 minutes
Servings: 4

3 tablespoons oleo
1 cup onion, chopped
3 cloves garlic, finely minced

1. In 2 quart dish, put oleo, onion and garlic. Micro on **High 3 Minutes.**

1 pint oysters
1/2 of oyster juice
6 drops Tabasco
2 bay leaves, crushed
1 teaspoon Rosemary
1/2 teaspoon oregano
2 teaspoons Worcestershire
    sauce
2 tablespoons lemon juice

2. Add oysters, juice, Tabasco, bay leaves, Rosemary, oregano, Worcestershire sauce and lemon juice. Micro on **High** about **7 Minutes,** or until oysters curl. Place in shells or ramekins and serve hot.

NOTE: 1/4 teaspoon Italian seasoning may be used in place of Rosemary and oregano.

TUNA MUSHROOM BAKE

Utensils: 2 cup glass measuring cup
6" x 8" casserole
Time: 12 minutes
Servings: 6

4 tablespoons oleo
1/2 cup celery, chopped
1/2 cup onion, chopped

1. In 2 cup measure, put oleo, celery and onion. Micro on **High 5 Minutes.**

1 large can (7 oz.) tuna, drained
1 can (4 oz.) Mushrooms and liquid
1 can (10 oz.) cream of celery soup
1/3 teaspoon black pepper
1/3 cup Italian bread crumbs

2. In oblong casserole, mix tuna, mushrooms and liquid, soup, pepper and bread crumbs. Add above onion-celery mixture. Mix well. Micro on **High 7 Minutes.** Sprinkle with 1 cup crushed potato chips or 1 can French Fried onion rings.

NOTE: For variety sprinkle with 1 cup crushed potato chips or with French Fried Onion Rings (canned).

SALMON IN TOMATO SAUCE

Utensils: 3 quart dish
Time: 41 minutes
Servings: 6

1/4 cup flour
1/4 cup oil

1. Roux: (See roux.) In 3 quart dish, put flour and oil. Micro on **High 6-7 Minutes, Until Brown.**

2/3 cup onion, chopped
1/2 cup celery, chopped

2. Add onion and celery. Micro on **High 5 Minutes.**

1/4 cup green onions, chopped
1/4 cup green pepper, chopped
1 can (16 oz.) tomatoes
1 can (16 oz.) salmon
2/3 cup water
1 can (8 oz.) tomato sauce
1 bay leaf
1/2 teaspoon Worcestershire sauce
1 tablespoon parsley flakes
— dash garlic powder
1/2 teaspoon cayenne pepper
1/4 teaspoon black pepper
1-1/2 teaspoons salt

3. Add green onions, green pepper tomatoes, salmon (remove round bone in salmon), water, tomato sauce, bay leaf, Worcestershire sauce, parsley, garlic, pepper and salt. Stir. Micro on **High 30 Minutes, Covered** with glass lid. Stir once or twice during cooking.

SEAFOOD BAKE

Utensils: 4 quart Corning dish
Time: 20 minutes
Servings: 10-12

**1 stick oleo or butter
   (8 tablespoons)**
1 cup green pepper, chopped
1 cup onion, chopped
1 cup green onion, chopped
1 cup celery, chopped

1/2 cup parsley, chopped
**2 cans (4 oz. each) mushroom
   pieces, drained**
1 pound white lump crabmeat
**2 cans (10 oz.) cream of mush-
   room soup**
**1 pint jar of oysters, chopped
   and drained (optional)**
**1 pound boiled shrimp,
   chopped**

1. In 4 quart casserole or dish, put oleo, green pepper, onion, green onions and celery. Micro on **High 10 Minutes** or until tender, **Uncovered.** Stir twice during cooking.

2. Add parsley, mushrooms, crab-meat, soup and oysters. Micro on **High 10 Minutes**, stirring once or twice. May be served as a casserole or a dip.

NOTE: If fresh jar oysters are not available, canned oysters may be used.

Vegetables

VEGETABLES

Vegetable Hints 96
Vegetable Cooking Charts 96, 97, 98
Delicious Artichokes 99
Baked Beans 99
Holland and French Beets Combo 100
Broccoli Chicken Casserole 101
Broccoli Rice Casserole 102
Shrimp and Broccoli Casserole 103
Beef and Cabbage Bake 104
Glorified Cabbage 105
Stuffed Cabbage Rolls 106
Cauliflower Au Gratin 107
Cauliflower La Bienville 108
Cauliflower Supreme 109
Corn and Tomato Creole 110
Corn on the Cob 110
Eggplant and Shrimp Casserole 111
Eggplant Parmesan 112
Cheesy Green Bean Casserole 113
Green Beans, French Style 114
Southern Field Peas 115
Tiny Green Peas, Southern Style 116
Baked Potatoes / Boiled / Sweet 117
Chili Potatoes 118
Smothered Potatoes, French Style 119
Italian Potatoes 120
Potatoes Anna 120
Pizza Potato Casserole 121
Potato Bake Casserole 122
Potatoes Au Gratin 123
Sour Cream Potato Casserole 124
Stuffed Potatoes A La New Orleans 125
Tuna Stuffed Potatoes 126
Creamed Spinach 127
Filled Acorn Squash/Pineapple or Cranberries 128
Summer Squash with Shrimp 129
Yam Praline Crunch 130
Creamy Yam Casserole 131
Zucchini Provolone 132

VEGETABLES

1. Vegetables cooked in your microwave oven retains its color, flavor and nutritional value.

2. **Vegetables** should be **Covered While Cooking** to retain moisture and steam.

3. **Fresh Vegetables** should be cooked with a **Small Amount of Water.**

4. **Frozen Vegetables** need **No Water** as ice crystals provide moisture.

5. **Frozen Vegetables** can be **Cooked Directly in Their Cartons.**

6. Vegetables can be cooked in pouches. The pouch should be slit before cooking to allow steam to escape.

7. **Most Vegetables** cook best on **Full Power** or **High.**

8. Vegetables **Should** still **Be a Little Firm** when removed from oven. They will continue cooking during standing time.

9. Vegetables should be **Cooked Until** they are **Fork Tender** or until **Desired Tenderness** is reached.

FROZEN VEGETABLE COOKING CHART

Vegetables should be cooked on **Full Power** for best results.

Vegetable	Amount	Cooking Procedure	Minutes On High
Asparagus, green spears	10 oz. pkg.	Separate after 3 min.	5 - 6
Beans, green cut or wax French cut	10 oz. pkg.	Add 2 tbsp. hot water Stir after 4 min.	7 - 8
Beans, green diagonal cut	10 oz. pouch	Slit pouch with knife	5 - 6
Beans, green French	10 oz. pouch	Slit pouch with knife	6 - 7
Beans, lima Fordhook	10 oz. pkg.	Add ¼ cup hot water Stir after 4 min.	8 - 9
Beans, lima	10 oz. pouch	Slit pouch with knife	6 - 7
Broccoli	10 oz. pkg.	Separate after 4 min.	8 - 9
Broccoli, spears	10 oz. pouch	Slit pouch with knife	6½ - 7½
Broccoli, in cheese sauce	10 oz. pouch	Slit pouch with knife	7½ - 8½
Brussel Sprouts	10 oz. pkg. 10 oz. pouch	Add 2 tbsp. hot water Slit pouch with knife	5 - 6 6 - 7
Carrots	10 oz. pkg.	Add 2 tbsp. hot water Stir after 3 min.	6 - 7
Carrots, nuggets	10 oz. pouch	Slit pouch with knife	6 - 7
Cauliflower	10 oz. pkg.	Add 2 tbsp. hot water	5 - 6

VEGETABLE

Cauliflower, in cheese sauce	10 oz. pouch	Slit pouch with knife	7½ - 8½
Corn, cut off cob	10 oz. pkg.	Add ¼ cup hot water	4 - 5
Corn, niblets and white shoe peg	10 oz. pouch	Slit pouch with knife	6 - 7
Corn, cream style	10 oz. pouch	Slit pouch with knife	5½ - 6½
Corn, on cob	1 ear	Place in small flat covered casserole	4 - 4½
	2 ears	Place in small flat covered casserole	6 - 7
	4 ears	Place in small flat covered casserole	10 - 11
Okra	10 oz. pkg.	Add 2 tbsp. hot water	6 - 7
Onions, in cream	10 oz. pouch	Slit pouch with knife	6 - 7
Peas, Black eyed	10 oz. pkg.	Add ¼ water	8 - 10
Peas, green	10 oz. pkg.	Add 2 tbsp. hot water	4½ - 5½
	10 oz. pouch	Slit pouch with knife	6 - 7
Peas & Carrots	10 oz. pkg.	Add 2 tbsp. hot water	5 - 6
Spinach, leaf or chopped	10 oz. pkg.	Add 2 tbsp. hot water	4½ - 5½
	10 oz. pouch	Slit pouch with knife	6½ - 7½
Squash, Hubbard	10 oz. pkg.	Add 2 tbsp. hot water	4 - 6
Vegetables, mixed	10 oz. pkg.	Add ¼ cup hot water	5 - 6
	10 oz. pouch	Slit pouch with knife	6 - 7

FRESH VEGETABLE COOKING CHART

Vegetable	Amount	Cooking Procedure	Minutes On HIGH
Artichokes	2 medium	Add 1/4 cup water	5-7
Asparagus	15 stalks (3/4 lb.)	Add 1/4 cup water	4-5
Beans, green	1 pound	Add 1/4 cup water	8-10
Beets (whole)	4 medium	Cover with water	16-17
*Broccoli	1 small bunch (1-1/2 lbs.)	Remove tough part of stalk. Split tender ends. Add 1/4 cup water.	8-9
Brussel Sprouts	1/2 lb. (2 cups)	Add 2 tablespoons water.	4-5
Cabbage	1 medium head	Wash, remove outer leaves, quarter and chop. Add 2 tablespoons water.	12-13

97

VEGETABLE

Carrots	4 medium sliced	Add 2 tablespoons water	6-7
*Cauliflower	1 medium head	Add 1/2 cup water	10-12
Celery	4 cups sliced (6 stalks)	Add 1/4 cup water	7-8
Eggplant	1 medium	Peel and dice. Add 1/4 cup water and 1/4 teaspoon salt.	5-6
Potatoes (boiled)	4 medium	Peel and quarter. Cover with hot water.	16-17
Rutabaga	1 lb.	Wash, peel and cube. Add 1/2 cup water. Stir during cooking.	8-9
Spinach	10 oz. package	Wash and remove thick stems. Shake off excess water.	5
Squash, Acorn	1 lb.	Pierce skin. Cook on paper plate.	7-8
Tomatoes	4 large	Clean, peel and halve. Add 2 tablespoons water.	4-6
Turnips	2 or 3 medium	Wash, peel and cube. Add 1/4 cup water. Stir after 5 minutes.	7-9
Zucchini or Summer Squash	2 medium	Cut into thin slices. Add 1 tablespoons water. Stir after 4 minutes.	6½-7½

*Fresh broccoli and whole cauliflower give excellent results on **70% Power** due to their density.

Broccoli (1-1/2 lbs.)	15 to 16 minutes	**70% Power**
Whole Cauliflower	12 to 15 minutes	**70% Power**

98

DELICIOUS ARTICHOKES

Utensils: 2-3 quart casserole or 8″ x 8″ square casserole
Time: 7 minutes
Time: 6-8

2 cans (8-1/2 oz.) artichokes, drained and cut in pieces (reserve 1/4 cup liquid)	1. Put artichokes in bottom of casserole.
1 cup Parmesan cheese 1 cup Italian bread crumbs	2. Mix cheese and bread crumbs. Sprinkle over artichokes.
1/2 cup oleo, melted 1/4 cup artichoke juice 1/4 cup olive oil	3. Micro oleo until melted. Add to juice and olive oil. Drizzle over top of casserole. Micro on **High 7 Minutes.**

BAKED BEANS

Utensils: 2 quart dish
Time: 26 minutes
Servings: 8

3 strips of bacon	1. In 2 quart dish, put bacon. Micro on **High about 3 Minutes,** or until bacon is crisp. Remove bacon. Crumble and set aside. Reserve bacon drippings in same dish.
1/4 cup onion, chopped 1/4 cup celery, chopped	2. In same dish, add onion and celery to bacon drippings. Micro on **High 3 Minutes, Uncovered.**
2 tablespoons green pepper, chopped 2 cans (16 oz.) Pork and Beans 1-1/4 tablespoons mustard 1/4 cup ketchup 4 tablespoons brown sugar 5 drops Tobasco (optional) 3-4 drops liquid smoke (optional) 1/4 cup water	3. Add crumbled bacon, green pepper, beans, mustard, ketchup, brown sugar, Tobasco, liquid smoke and water. Micro on **High 5 Minutes,** then on **70% Power for 15 Minutes, Uncovered** until thick. Let stand 5 minutes, covered.

HOLLAND AND FRENCH BEETS COMBO

Utensils: 2 quart dish
Time: 2 minutes, 30 seconds
Servings: 6

2 tablespoons flour
1 tablespoon sugar
2 tablespoons lemon juice
1 tablespoon onion,
   chopped fine
3 tablespoons butter or oleo,
   melted
beet juice

1 can (16 oz.) beets, drained,
   (reserve juice)

1.   In 2 quart dish, mix flour, sugar, lemon juice, onion, butter and beet juice. (Add beet juice a little at a time, stirring.) Micro on **High about 2 Minutes, Uncovered,** until thickened.   Stir   to   prevent lumping.

2.   Add beets and Micro on **High 30 Seconds.** Stir.

NOTE: For variation, omit onions and add 4 boiled eggs, cut in halves.

BROCCOLI CHICKEN CASSEROLE

Utensils: 3 or 4 quart deep casserole dish
2 quart bowl
7" x 11" oblong casserole dish
Time: 43 minutes
Servings: 8

**4-6 chicken breasts or
6 chicken thighs
2 cups water**

1. In 3 quart dish, put water and chicken parts. Cover. Micro on **High 20-30 Minutes** or until tender. Drain. Reserve chicken broth. Remove meat from bone and chop into chunks.

**2 packages (10 oz.) frozen
broccoli
1/4 cup water**

2. In 2 quart bowl, put broccoli and water. Cover. Micro on **High 10-12 Minutes.** Drain and chop.

**2 cans (10 oz.) cream of
chicken soup
1 tablespoon lemon juice
1 cup Cheez Whiz
(processed cheese
spread) or Cheddar
cheese, grated
2/3 cup Mayonnaise
Salt and pepper to taste
1/3 cup chicken broth**

3. In 2 quart bowl, put soup, lemon juice, cheese, mayonnaise, salt, pepper and chicken broth. Micro on **High 3-4 Minutes,** (stirring) or until cheese is melted. Fold in chicken.

**1/4 cup bread crumbs
(plain)**

4. In oblong casserole, put a layer of broccoli, then a layer of chicken sauce. Repeat. Sprinkle with bread crumbs. Dot with butter. Micro on **High 10 Minutes, Uncovered.**

101

BROCCOLI RICE CASSEROLE

Utensils: 2 quart bowl
           10" Browning skillet or 3 quart dish
Time: 32 minutes
Servings: 6

1 package (10 oz.) frozen broccoli
1/4 cup water

1. In 2 quart bowl, put broccoli and water. Micro on **High 7 Minutes, Covered.** Drain and chop. Set aside.

3 tablespoons oleo
1 cup onion, chopped (1 medium onion)
1/2 cup celery, chopped

2. In 10" skillet or 3 quart dish, put oleo, onions and celery. Micro on **High 6 Minutes, Uncovered.**

1 can (10 oz.) cream of chicken soup
1 small can (5 oz.) evaporated milk
1 small jar (8 oz.) Cheez Whiz (processed cheese spread)

3. Add soup, evaporated milk and Cheez Whiz. Micro on **High 7 Minutes, Covered,** stirring.

1/2 teaspoon salt
1/4 teaspoon cayenne pepper
1/4 teaspoon black pepper
2 cups cooked rice

4. Add salt, cayenne and black pepper, rice and cooked broccoli. Micro on **High 10-12 Minutes, stirring (especially around sides), Uncovered.**

1/4 cup plain bread crumbs

5. Sprinkle with bread crumbs. Micro on **High 2 Minutes, Uncovered.**

SHRIMP BROCCOLI CASSEROLE

Utensils: 2-1/2 quart deep dish casserole
7" x 11" oblong casserole dish
Time: 36 minutes
Servings: 8

2 packages (10 oz.) frozen broccoli spears
1/2 cup water

1. In 2-1/2 quart dish, put broccoli and watr. Micro on **High 12-14 Minutes, Covered** with lid or plastic wrap. Drain and chop. Set aside.

1/2 cup oleo
1 cup onion, chopped
1/2 cup green bell pepper, chopped
2/3 cup celery, chopped

2. In same 2-1/2 quart dish, put oleo, onion, green pepper and celery. Micro on **High 9 Minutes,** or until saute'ed.

1 to 1-1/2 pounds shrimp, par-boiled (boiled just until pink). peeled and chopped
2 cans (4 oz.) mushroom pieces, drained

3. Add shrimp and mushroom pieces. Micro on **High About 8 Minutes, Covered.** Stir once or twice during cooking.

1 can (10-3/4 oz.) cream of mushroom soup
1 jar (8 oz.) Cheez Whiz (processed cheese spread)
2 teaspoons salt
1/2 teaspoon cayenne pepper
1/2 teaspoon black pepper
1/2 teaspoon garlic powder

4. Add soup, cheese, salt, pepper and garlic powder. Micro on **High 3 Minutes,** until cheese melts.

2/3 cup plain bread crumbs

5. Stir in chopped broccoli and bread crumbs. Put into 7" x 11" oblong dish. Micro on **High 4. Minutes, Uncovered.**

NOTE: May be used as a dip.
NOTE: Shrimp may be omitted.

BEEF AND CABBAGE BAKE

Utensils: 4 quart Corning casserole
Time: 88 minutes
Servings: 8-10

1 medium cabbage, chopped
3 cups Hot water

1. In 4 quart casserole, put cabbage and water. Micro on **High 20 Minutes, Covered.** Drain and set aside.

1 cup onion, chopped
1 cup celery, chopped
1/2 cup green pepper,
   chopped

2. In same dish, put onion, celery and green pepper. Micro on **High 13 Minutes.**

1 pound ground beef

3. Add ground beef. Micro on **High 10 Minutes,** stirring and mashing. (use a potato masher if available).

1 can (10-1/2 oz.) Ro-Tel
   tomatoes

4. Add tomatoes and cabbage. Micro on **High 40 Minutes, Covered,** stirring occasionally.

1/3 cup plain bread crumbs
1/3 cup Italian bread crumbs
salt to taste

5. Add bread crumbs and salt.

1/4 cup (any kind)
   bread crumbs

6. Sprinkle with 1/4 cup crumbs. Micro on **High 5 Minutes.**

NOTE: For something different this is an excellent dish.

GLORIFIED CABBAGE

Utensils: 4 quart Corning dish
Time: 48 minutes
Servings: 6-8

1 medium head of cabbage, chopped
1/2 cup water

1. In 4 quart dish, put cabbage and water. Cover with lid or plastic wrap. Micro on **High 25-30 Minutes,** until very tender. Stir once during cooking. Drain and set aside.

6 tablespoons butter or oleo
1 small onion or 1/2 cup onion, chopped

2. In 4 quart Corning dish, put oleo and onion. Micro on **High 4 Minutes.**

1 can (10-3/4 oz.) cream of mushroom soup
1/2 pound Velveeta cheese, cut in chunks (about 1-2/3 cups) or Cheez Whiz spread.

3. Add soup and cheese. Micro on **High 4 Minutes** or until cheese is melted.

2/3 cup unseasoned bread crumbs
1 teaspoon salt
1/2 teaspoon cayenne pepper

4. Add bread crumbs and cabbage, salt and pepper. Mix well. Put in 4 quart dish. Sprinkle with more bread crumbs. Micro on **70% Power 15 Minutes, Covered.**

NOTE: Any other favorite cheese may be substituted.

STUFFED CABBAGE ROLLS

Utensils: 3 quart deep dish
Large bowl
Small bowl
Time: 67 minutes
Servings: 10-12

1 medium cabbage
1/4 cup water

1. Discard top leaves of cabbage. Put cabbage and water in 3 quart dish. Cover with lid or plastic wrap. Micro on **High 12 Minutes.** Drain and cool.

1-1/2 pounds ground beef
*1 can (10 oz.) Ro Tel tomatoes
salt to taste
1/2 cup Italian bread crumbs
1/4 cup Parmesan cheese
1 egg
1 teaspoon parsley flakes

2. In large bowl, mix ground beef, tomatoes and juice, salt, bread crumbs, Parmesan cheese, egg and parsley.

2 tablespoons oleo
1/4 cup celery, chopped
1/4 cup green pepper,
chopped
1/2 cup onion, chopped

3. In small bowl, put oleo, onion, celery and green pepper. Micro on **High 5 Minutes.** Add to meat mixture and mix well. Loosen cabbage leaves. If leaves are large cut in half. Put a scoop of meat mixture on each leaf. Roll up. Place in 4 quart casserole. (Roll about 20-25 leaves.) Put aside remainder of meat mixture and cabbage leaves.

3 cans (8 oz.) tomato sauce
1 can (6 oz.) V-8 juice
1 can (10 oz.) tomatoes
1 cup cabbage leaves,
chopped
salt and pepper to taste
remainder of ground beef
mixture

4. Mix tomato sauce, V-8 juice, tomatoes, chopped cabbage, salt, pepper and remainder of ground beef. Pour over cabbage rolls. Micro on **High 40 Minutes, Covered** with lid or plastic wrap, and then on **High 10 Minutes, Covered** with wax paper.

NOTE: Regular canned tomatoes may be substituted for Ro Tel tomatoes. If regular canned tomatoes are used then pepper has to be added to meat mixture.

CAULIFLOWER AU GRATIN

Utensils: 3 quart casserole
Time: 24 minutes
Servings: 6

2 packages (10 oz.) frozen cauliflower
1/2 cup water

1. In 3 quart casserole, put cauliflower and water. Micro on **High 12 Minutes, Covered.** Let stand 3 minutes. Drain. Set aside.

1/3 cup butter or oleo
1/3 cup onion, chopped

2. In 3 quart casserole, put butter and onion. Micro on **High 3 Minutes, Uncovered.**

1-1/4 cups Cheddar cheese, grated
1/4 cup milk
1 can (10 oz.) Cream of mushroom soup

3. Add cheese, milk and soup. Micro on **High 5 Minutes.** Stir once or twice during cooking. Add cauliflower. Stir. You may put in 7" x 11" casserole or leave in 3 quart dish.

1/2 cup Italian bread crumbs
1/3 cup Parmesan cheese

4. Sprinkle with bread crumbs, then cheese. Micro on **High 4 Minutes.** Serve hot.

CAULIFLOWER LA BIENVILLE

Utensils: 3 quart deep dish casserole
2 quart small casserole dish
Time: 30 minutes
Servings: 6

2 packages (10 oz.) frozen
cauliflower, or
1 medium cauliflower (whole)
1/2 cup water

1. In 3 quart dish, put whole cauliflower in water. Cover and Micro
on **High 12-14 Minutes** or until
tender. Drain. (10 minutes for
frozen cauliflower.)

1 cup onion, chopped
4 tablespoons butter

2. In 2 quart dish, put onion and
butter. Micro on **High 3 Minutes,
Uncovered.**

1 can (4 oz.) mushroom pieces,
drained or 1-1/2 cups
fresh mushrooms, cut

3. Add mushrooms to onions. Micro
on **High 3 Minutes, Uncovered.**

1 pound raw shrimp, peeled
and chopped
salt and pepper to taste
— dash garlic powder

4. Add shrimp, salt, pepper and
garlic powder to mushroom
mixture. Micro on **High 5 Minutes,
Uncovered.**

1 can (10-3/4 oz.) cream of
mushroom soup
1-1/4 cups mild Cheddar
cheese or
1 cup sharp Cheddar cheese,
grated

5. Add soup and cheese. Micro on
High 5 Minutes. Mixture will be
thick. Stir once or twice during
cooking. Pour over cauliflower
and sprinkle with paprika. Serve
hot.

NOTE: Boiled shrimp may be used in place of raw; if so, omit cooking
time in step 4.

CAULIFLOWER SUPREME

Utensils: 3 quart casserole or dish
            8″ x 8″ square dish
Time: 17 minutes
Servings: 8

**2 packages (10 oz.) frozen
   cauliflower
1/2 cup water**

1. In 3 quart dish, put cauliflower and water. Micro on **High 12 Minutes, Covered.** Drain. Arrange cauliflower in square dish.

1/2 cup oleo, melted

2. Pour oleo over cauliflower and mix to coat.

**2/3 cup Swiss or Cheddar
   cheese, grated
1/3 cup Parmesan cheese
1/4 cup Italian bread crumbs**

3. Combine cheeses and crumbs and sprinkle over cauliflower. Micro on **High 5 Minutes, Uncovered.**

109

CORN AND TOMATO CREOLE

Utensils: 2 quart dish or casserole
4 cup glass measuring cup
Time: 27 minutes
Servings: 6

2 tablespoons oil
2 tablespoons flour

1. Roux: (See Roux.) In 4 cup measuring cup, put oil and flour. Micro on **High 4-5 Minutes,** until golden brown. Stir roux when starting to get brown and every 30 seconds after until desired color is obtained.

1/4 cup onion, chopped
1-1/2 tablespoons green pepper, chopped

2. Add onion and green pepper. Micro on **High 2-3 Minutes.**

1 can (16 oz.) whole corn and liquid
1 can (15 oz.) tomato sauce
2-1/2 tablespoons sugar
1/4 teaspoon salt
1/4 teaspoon cayenne pepper

3. Put corn and liquid, tomato sauce, sugar, salt, pepper and roux in 2 quart dish. Micro on **50% Power 20 Minutes, Uncovered,** or if wish to prevent splatter, cover with wax paper.

CORN ON THE COB

Utensils: Flat casserole dish

FROZEN: Micro on High

Put corn in dish and cover or wrap in wax paper. Add butter before or after cooked.

1 ear — 4-1/2 Minutes
2 ears — 6-7 MInutes
4 ears — 10-11 Minutes

FRESH: Husk corn and wash. Micro on High.

Put corn in dish. Add melted butter or margarine and cover or wrap in wax paper.

2 ears — 4 Minutes
4 ears — 8 Minutes
6 ears — 12 Minutes

EGGPLANT AND SHRIMP CASSEROLE

Utensils: 4 or 5 quart casserole dish
             3 quart dish
Time: 46 minutes
Servings: 4

**3 medium eggplants, peeled
  and diced
1/4 cup water**

1. Put eggplant and water in 4 or 5 quart casserole dish. Micro on **High 25 Minutes** or until very tender, **Covered** with lid or plastic wrap. Drain.

**1/2 cup onion, chopped
1/4 cup oil**

2. In 3 quart dish, put onion and oil. Micro on **High 3 Minutes, Uncovered.**

**1 pound raw shrimp, peeled
  and chopped**

3. Add shrimp to onion. Micro on **High 3 Minutes, Uncovered.** Stir once or twice.

**1/2 teaspoon parsley flakes or
  2 tablespoons fresh
  parsley, chopped
salt, black pepper and cayenne
  pepper to taste
— dash of garlic powder**

4. Return to 4 quart casserole dish the eggplant and the shrimp mixture. Add parsley, salt, pepper and garlic powder. Micro on **High 5 Minutes,** then on **70% Power 10 more Minutes, Uncovered.** Stir occasionally. Make sure eggplant is well seasoned for a zesty flavor. Serve with rice.

NOTE: Variation 1:   Before last 10 minutes of cooking, eggplant may be sprinkled with 1 cup of Italian bread crumbs, then 1/2 cup of Parmesan cheese.

NOTE: Variation 2:   1 can or 1 pound of white lump crabmeat may be added before last 10 minutes of cooking time.

NOTE: Variation 3: For stuffed eggplant—cut eggplants in half and cook as in step 1. Scoop out centers and proceed with remaining steps 2 and 3. Mix ingredients as in step 4 and stuff mixture into shells, then proceed with cooking as in step 4.

111

EGGPLANT PARMESAN

Utensils: 4 quart Corning dish or similar
            2 small mixing bowls
            7" x 11" oblong casserole dish
Time: 27 minutes
Servings: 6-8

**3 small eggplants, peeled
   and cubed
2 cups water**

1. In 4 quart dish, put eggplant and water. Cover. Micro on **High 15-20 Minutes,** until tender. Drain. Set aside.

**2/3 cup Parmesan cheese
2/3 cup Italian bread crumbs
2/3 cup plain bread crumbs**

2. In small mixing bowl, mix together tomato sauce, Italian seasoning, garlic powder, salt and pepper. Set aside.

**3 cans (8 oz.) tomato sauce
1 teaspoon Italian seasoning
1/4 teaspoon garlic powder
1/2 teaspoon salt
1/4 teaspoon cayenne pepper**

3. In small mixing bowl, mix together Parmesan cheese, Italian bread crumbs, and plain bread crumbs. Set aside.

2/3 cup Parmesan cheese

4. In 7" x 11" oblong casserole, put a layer of eggplant, a layer of breadcrumbs, a layer of tomato sauce and a layer of Parmesan cheese. Repeat two more times. Micro on **High 10 Minutes.**

**1 package (4 oz.) Mozzarella
   or Cheddar cheese,
   grated**

5. Sprinkle with cheese. Micro on **High 2 Minutes,** until cheese melts.

CHEESY GREEN BEAN CASSEROLE

Utensils: 2-1/2 to 3 quart casserole dish
Time: 14 minutes
Servings: 8

4 tablespoons oleo
1/2 cup onion, chopped

1. In 3 quart dish, put oleo and onions. Micro on **High 3 Minutes, Uncovered.** Stir once.

1 can (4 oz.) chopped mushrooms, drained well
2-1/2 tablespoons flour
1/2 cup evaporated milk
1-1/4 cups Cheddar cheese, grated
2 cans French Style green beans, drained
1 teaspoon soy sauce
1/2 teaspoon salt
1/2 teaspoon monosodium glutamate
1 (2 or 3 oz.) can water chestnuts, drained and sliced (optional)

2. Add mushrooms and flour and stir. Add milk and stir. Add cheese, green beans, soy sauce, salt, monosodium glutamate and water chestnuts. Stir. Micro on **High 8 Minutes, Covered** with lid or plastic wrap.

1/3 can French Fried Onion Rings

3. Sprinkle with onion rings. Micro on **High 3 Minutes, Uncovered.**

NOTE: For variety 1 can of cream of mushroom soup may be substituted in the place of the flour and milk.

GREEN BEANS FRENCH STYLE

Utensils: 10″ browning skillet or 3 quart Corning or casserole dish
Time: 29 minutes
Servings: 6

2 tablespoons oil
1/2 cup onion, chopped

1. In browning skillet or casserole dish, put oil and onion. Micro on **High 3 Minutes.**

1/2 pound of hot sausage,
  smoked sausage,
  chopped, or ham chunks

2. Add sausage or ham. Micro on **High 1 Minute, Uncovered.**

2 cans (15 oz.) French Style
  green beans, drained
3 medium potatoes, cut
  in quarters
1/2 teaspoon salt
pepper to taste
— dash of garlic powder

3. Add green beans, potatoes, salt, pepper and garlic powder. Micro on **High 20 Minutes, Covered,** stirring occasionally. **Uncover** and Micro on **High 5 Minutes,** stirring once or twice. Potatoes should be tender at end of cooking time. Cover and let stand about 5 minutes.

SOUTHERN FIELD PEAS

Utensils: 1-1/2 to 2 quart Corning dish or other, same size
Time: 24 minutes
Servings: 4-6

2 tablespoons oil
2 tablespoons flour

1. Roux: (See Roux) In Corning dish, put oil and flour. Micro on **High 4-5 Minutes,** or until roux is golden brown. Stir roux as it begins to brown and stir every 30 seconds after until desired color is obtained.

1/3 cup onion, chopped
2 tablespoons green onions, chopped
2 tablespoons green pepper, chopped (may use pepper flakes)

2. Add onion, green onions and green pepper. Micro on **High 4 Minutes, Uncovered.**

2/3 cup Hot Sausage, Smoked Sausage or ham, chopped
1 can (15 oz.) field peas (not cream style)
1/2 cup hot water
1/2 teaspoon parsley or parsley flakes
1/2 teaspoon salt
1/4 teaspoon black pepper
cayenne pepper to taste (see note)
— dash garlic powder

3. Add sausage or ham, peas and their liquid, water, parsley, salt, pepper and garlic powder. Micro on **High 10 Minutes,** then Micro on **70% Power 5 Minutes, Uncovered.**

NOTE: If using Hot Sausage, do not use any pepper.

115

TINY GREEN PEAS SOUTHERN STYLE
(Petit Pois Peas)

Utensils: 1-1/2 to 2 quart Corning or Pyrex dish
Time: 20-22 minutes
Servings: 4-6

2 tablespoons oil
2 tablespoons flour

1. Roux: In 2 quart dish, put oil and flour. Micro on **High 3-5 Minutes,** until **very light** brown. Stir.

1/4 cup onion, chopped

2. Add onion. Micro on **High 2 Minutes, Uncovered.**

1 can (16 oz.) tiny green peas
**   (do not drain)**
1 tablespoon butter or oleo
1 tablespoon sugar
1/4 teaspoon salt
— dash cayenne pepper
— dash black pepper
1/2 cup hot water

3. Add peas and their water, butter, sugar, salt, pepper and hot water. Micro on **70% Power 5 Minutes, Uncovered.** Stir. Micro on **High 8- 10 Minutes, Uncovered,** until thick.

NOTE: If desired this recipe can be doubled. Double everything but the hot water. Use only 1/2 cup hot water. Use following time: Oil and Flour — Micro on **High 3-5 Minutes,** until very light brown. Add Onions — Micro on **High 3 Minutes.** Remainder of ingredients — Micro on **High 18-20 Minutes** or until thick, **Uncovered.**

NOTE: If a spicier taste is desired add more salt and pepper.

BAKED POTATOES

Select potatoes which are equal in size. Wash and pierce with fork in several paces. Place potatoes in a flat dish or on paper towels. For time use the following chart. Turn potato over half way during cooking time. Remove potato from oven. Wrap in foil. Let stand about 5 minutes.

1 medium potato	**4-6 minutes on HIGH**
1 large potato	**5-6 minutes on HIGH**
2 medium potatoes	**6-8 minutes on HIGH**
4 medium potatoes	**12-15 minutes on HIGH**

BOILED POTATOES

Wash potatoes and cut in half. Cover with water in a 2-1/2 quart dish. Cover with lid or plastic wrap. Follow chart below:

4 medium potatoes	**10-12 minutes on HIGH**

SWEET POTATOES

Prepare as you would regular potatoes.

NOTE: The above charts are for ovens of 650 wattage. If your oven is over 650 wattage or one of the following ovens (Litton, Amana, Magic Chef), the time required may be a little less.

CHILI POTATOES

Utensils: Round Microwave cake pan or 3 quart Pyrex dish
Time: 23 minutes
Servings: 4-6

3 slices bacon

1. In cake pan or dish, Micro bacon on **High 3 Minutes.** Remove bacon. Crumble and set aside.

1 cup onion, chopped

2. Add onion and Micro on **High about 5 Minutes.**

6 medium potatoes, peeled and sliced
2 teaspoons chili powder
2 tablespoons oleo
salt and pepper to taste

3. Add potatoes, chili powder, oleo, salt and pepper. Micro on **High 15-18 Minutes,** until tender, **Covered** with plastic wrap or glass cover. Stir once or twice during cooking. Add crumbled bacon. Serve hot.

NOTE: Potatoes must be stirred during cooking to prevent dehydration around the edges.

NOTE: Bacon may be omitted. If so, use 2 tablespoons oil in Step 2 in place of bacon fat.

SMOTHERED POTATOES FRENCH STYLE

Utensils: 3 quart dish
Time: 21-26 minutes
Servings: 6

6 medium potatoes, peeled and diced

1. Prepare potatoes and set aside.

1/2 cup onion, chopped
2 tablespoons oil

2. In 3 quart dish, put oil and onion. Micro on **High 3 Minutes, Uncovered.**

1/4 cup green onions, chopped

3. Add green onions. Micro on **High 3 Minutes, Uncovered.**

salt and pepper to taste

4. Add potatoes, salt and pepper. Micro on **High 15-20 Minutes, Covered** with lid or plastic wrap. (Until tender.) Stir during cooking.

NOTE: Cooking time for potatoes depends on size.

NOTE: Since vegetables dehydrate when overcooked, they must be stirred during cooking to prevent uneven cooking around outer edge of dish.

119

VEGETABLE

ITALIAN POTATOES

Utensils: Round Microwave dish or 3 quart Pyrex dish
Time: 18 minutes
Servings: 6

6 medium potatoes, sliced

1. Put potatoes in Microwave cake dish or 3 quart casserole.

6 tablespoons butter or oleo, melted
1 teaspoon McCormick Italian Seasoning
1/4 teaspoon garlic powder
1/4 teaspoon black pepper
— dash of cayenne pepper
1/2 teaspoon salt

2. Mix oleo, Italian Seasoning, garlic powder, pepper and salt. Pour over potatoes. Micro on **High 16-18 Minutes** or until very tender. Stirring occasionally. Cook covered with a round Pyrex cover or plastic wrap. Stir once or twice during cooking.

VARIATION OF ABOVE:

POTATOES ANNA

Utensils: same as above
Time: 18 minutes
Servings: 6

6 medium potatoes, sliced
6 tablespoons butter or oleo, melted
salt and pepper to taste

1. Put potatoes in Microwave cake dish or 3 quart casserole. Add oleo, salt and pepper. Micro on **High 16-18 Minutes,** or until tender, stirring occasionally. Cover with a round Pyrex cover or plastic wrap. Stir once or twice during cooking.

NOTE: Potatoes must be stirred during cooking to prevent dehydration around the edges.

PIZZA POTATO CASSEROLE

Utensils: 3 quart dish and lid
7" x 11" casserole or similar
4 cup glass measuring cup or similar
Time: 28 minutes
Servings: 6

4 medium or large potatoes
salt and pepper to taste

1. Scrub potatoes with water. Micro on **High about 15 Minutes,** until potatoes are tender. Let cool and peel. Slice thickly and put in 7" x 11" casserole. Sprinkle with salt and pepper.

2 tablespoons oleo
1/2 cup green onions,
   chopped fine
1/2 pound Hot Sausage,
   Smoked Sausage or
   Italian Sausage, sliced
   thin

2. In 4 cup glass measuring cup, put oleo, green onions and sausage. Micro on **High 3 Minutes, Uncovered.**

2-1/2 cups Cheddar cheese,
   grated
1/4 teaspoon oregano
1/4 teaspoon basil

3. Add cheese, oregano and basil to onion and sausage. Mix.

2 tomatoes, sliced

4. In 7" x 11" casserole, top potatoes with half of cheese and sausage mixture. Top with tomato slices. Top with remainder of cheese and sausage. Micro on **High 5 Minutes, Uncovered,** then Micro on **70% Power 5 Minutes, Uncovered.**

POTATO BAKE CASSEROLE

Utensils: 3 quart deep dish casserole
7" x 11" oblong casserole dish
Time: 20 minutes
Servings: 6

**8 medium potatoes, peeled
  and cut in fourths**
1/2 cup water

1. In 3 quart dish, put potatoes and water. Cover with lid. If no lid, use plastic wrap. Micro on **High 15-18 Minutes** or until potatoes are tender. Let stand 5 minutes. Drain and mash.

1 egg, slightly beaten
**1 carton (8 oz.) sour cream or
  1 package sour cream mix
  (mixed according to
  directions on package)**
1 teaspoon salt
1/4 teaspoon cayenne pepper
1/4 teaspoon black pepper
1/4 cup onion, chopped finely

2. In 7" x 11" casserole, mix together egg, sour cream, salt, pepper and onion. Mix in mashed potatoes.

1/4 cup Parmesan cheese
1/2 cup Italian bread crumbs

3. Sprinkle with Parmesan cheese, then Italian bread crumbs. Micro on **High 5 Minutes.**

POTATOES AU GRATIN

Utensils: 8″ or 9″ pie dish or microwave cake pan
Time: 16-18 minutes
Sevings: 4-6

**6 to 8 medium potatoes,
    peeled and sliced
1 block oleo (8 tablespoons)**

1. In pie dish, put oleo and potatoes. Micro on **High 13-18 Minutes,** or until tender, **Covered** with pyrex cover or plastic wrap. Stir occasionally. (See note.)

**1/2 cup milk
1 can (10-3/4 oz.) cream of
    mushroom soup
1 cup sharp Cheddar cheese,
    grated
1/2 teaspoon salt
1/8 teaspoon black pepper**

2. In small dish mix milk, soup, cheese, salt and pepper. Micro on **High 4 Minutes** or until cheese melts. Mix with potatoes. Micro on **High 2 More Minutes, Uncovered.**

**1 can (3 oz.) French Fried Onion
    Rings, crushed (optional)**

3. Sprinkle onion rings over potatoes. Serve hot.

NOTE: Time of baking potatoes differs on the amount of potatoes and the size. Make sure potatoes are tender before removing from oven.

NOTE: Potatoes must be stirred during cooking to prevent dehydration around edges.

SOUR CREAM POTATO CASSEROLE

Utensils: 3 quart dish
              8" x 8" square dish
Time: 20-23 minutes
Servings: 6

6 medium potatoes
1 cup water

1. In 3 quart dish, put potatoes and water. Cover with lid. If no lid then use plastic wrap. Micro on **High 15-18 Minutes, depending on the size of potatoes.** Stick a two prong fork through potatoes to see when done. Fork should go through. Let stand 5 minutes, covered. Drain, cool and peel. Cut into chunks and put into 8" x 8" square dish.

1 carton (8 oz.) sour cream
1-1/4 cups Cheddar cheese,
**   grated**
2 teaspoons chives

2. Mix sour cream, cheese and chives with potatoes. Micro on **High 8 Minutes,** or until cheese is bubbly throughout.

NOTE: 2 or 3 tablespoons finely chopped green onions may be substituted in the place of chives.

STUFFED POTATOES A LA NEW ORLEANS

Utensils: 8" x 8" square dish
          Small dish
Time: 17 minutes
Servings: 4

2 medium baking potatoes

1. Bake potatoes in Microwave oven until slightly soft to touch. **(6-8 Minutes on High).** (See baked potatoes). Let stand 5 minutes, covered, until tender. Scoop out center and place in small dish. Mash.

4 strips bacon

2. In another small dish, Micro bacon on **High 3-4 Minutes,** until crisp. Remove and crumble. Set aside. Reserve 3 tablespoons bacon fat in same dish.

1/4 cup shallots (green onions), or onions, chopped

3. In reserved bacon fat, add shallots or onions. Micro on **High 3 Minutes.** Drain off all fat or oil.

2 tablespoons Parmesan cheese
1/2 cup sour cream
1/2 teaspoon salt
1/2 teaspoon black pepper

4. Mix together potatoes, bacon, onion, cheese, sour cream, salt and pepper. Stuff into potato shells. Sprinkle with parsley flakes and paprika. Place in 8" x 8" square dish. Micro on **High 3 Minutes.** Serve hot.

TUNA STUFFED POTATOES

Utensils: Glass serving platter
2 quart dish
Time: 17 minutes
Servings: 8

4 medium baking potatoes

1. Bake potatoes in Microwave until slightly soft to touch. **(13-15 Minutes on High)** (See baked potatoes). Let stand about 5 minutes covered with foil, or until tender throughout. Scoop out centers and place centers in 2 quart dish. Set potato shells aside.

3/4 cup mayonnaise
1/2 cup Cheddar cheese, grated
1/4 cup pimento, chopped (optional)
1/4 cup onion, finely chopped or 1 tablespoon minced onion (dried)
2 small cans tuna, drained
salt and pepper to taste

2. Mash potato centers. Mix in mayonnaise, cheese, pimento, onion, tuna, salt and pepper. Spoon mixture back into shells. Spread with topping. Micro on **High 4-6 Minutes,** depending on size of potatoes, or until heated through. (Micro and serve on glass serving platter.)

TOPPING:
1/4 cup mayonnaise
3/4 cup Cheddar cheese, grated

3. Mix together mayonnaise and cheese in small bowl.

NOTE: If a milder tuna taste is desired, you may use one can instead of two.

CREAMED SPINACH

Utensils: 3 quart dish or casserole
Time: 21 minutes
Servings: 6-8

2 cans (15 oz.) spinach, drained, or 2 packs frozen spinach

1. If using frozen spinach, Micro on **High 12 Minutes.** Drain.

4 tablespoons oleo, melted
2 tablespoons onion, chopped

2. In 3 quart dish, put oleo and onion. Micro on **High 2 Minutes.**

2 tablespoons flour
1/2 cup evaporated milk
1/3 cup water

3. Stir in flour, add milk and water slowly. Micro on **High 2 Minutes.**

1 jar (8 oz.) Cheez Whiz (processed cheese spread)

4. Add cheese and Micro on **High about 1 Minute** or until cheese is melted.

1/4 teaspoon garlic powder
1/2 teaspoon celery salt (optional)
1/2 teaspoon black pepper
1/3 teaspoon cayenne pepper
1 teaspoon Worcestershire sauce
1/4 cup Italian bread crumbs

5. Add garlic powder, celery salt, pepper, Worcestershire sauce and spinach. Sprinkle with bread crumbs. Micro on **High 4 Minutes.**

ACORN SQUASH
FILLED WITH CRANBERRIES
(Perfect For A Brunch)

Utensils: Shallow baking dish
Time: 18 minutes
Servings: 4

2 small acorn squash
4 tablespoons butter
4 tablespoons honey or
  brown sugar
1 can (16 oz.) whole-berry
  cranberry sauce

1. Cut squash in half. Place on paper towels in oven. Micro on **High 13-15 Minutes,** or until tender. (Prick through with a two prong fork.) Scoop out seeds. Put 1 tablespoon honey or brown sugar in each half. Place in shallow baking dish. Micro on **High 2 Minutes.** Fill each half with cranberry sauce. Micro on **High 2-4 Minutes,** until hot.

ACORN SQUASH
FILLED WITH PINEAPPLE

Utensils: Shallow baking dish
Time: 18 minutes
Servings: 4

2 small acorn squash
1 small can (8 oz.) crushed
  pineapple, drained
1/2 cup brown sugar
1/4 teaspoon cinnamon
1/4 teaspoon nutmeg
1/4 cup chopped pecans
4 tablespoons oleo

1. Cut squash in half. Place on paper towels in oven. Micro on **High 13-15 Minutes,** or until tender. (Prick through with a two prong fork.) Scoop out seeds. Mix together pineapple, brown sugar, cinnamon, nutmeg, pecans and oleo. Put mixture into squash halves. Micro on **High 3-4 Minutes,** until bubbly and hot.

NOTE: For another variation of Squash Filled with Pineapple: omit pineapple.

128

SUMMER SQUASH WITH SHRIMP

Utensils: 4 quart Corning casserole dish
3 quart deep dish casserole
Time: 60 minutes
Servings: 6

4 large white summer squash, peeled and diced
1/4 cup water

1. In 4 quart Corning dish, put squash and water. Cover with lid or plastic wrap. Micro on **High about 20 Minutes** or until tender. Drain.

2 tablespoons oil
1/2 cup onion, chopped
2 tablespoons green onions, chopped

2. In 3 quart dish, put oil, onion and green onions. Micro on **High 3-5 Minutes** or until sauteed.

1 to 1-1/2 pounds raw shrimp, peeled and chopped

3. Add shrimp and Micro on **High 5 Minutes, Covered** with lid.

1 teaspoon parsley flakes or 2 tablespoons fresh parsley, chopped
2 teaspoons salt
1/4 teaspoon black pepper
1/4 teaspoon cayenne pepper
— dash garlic powder

4. To shrimp mixture, add squash, parsley, salt, pepper and garlic powder. Mix well. Micro on **70% Power 20 Minutes,** then on **50% Power 10 Minutes, Uncovered.** Stir at intervals during cooking.

NOTE: If casserole effect is desired: the last 10 minutes of cooking put in flat casserole dish and sprinkle with bread crumbs.

YAM PRALINE CRUNCH

Utensils: 6" x 8" or 8" x 8" casserole dish
Time: 10 minutes
Servings: 6

**1 can (28 oz.) yams, drained
  and mashed
1/4 teaspoon salt
1/4 cup butter or oleo
2 eggs, slightly beaten
1 teaspoon vanilla
1/2 teaspoon cinnamon
1/2 cup sugar**

1. In casserole dish, put mashed yams, salt, butter, eggs, vanilla, cinnamon and sugar. Mix well. Sprinkle with topping. (See note.) Micro on **High 8 Minutes.**

TOPPING: (See Note)

**3 tablespoons oleo
3 tablespoons flour
3/4 cup dark brown or medium
  dark brown sugar
3/4 - 1 cup pecans, chopped**

2. In small bowl, mix all ingredients until oleo is mixed in thoroughly. Sprinkle over yams.

NOTE: If you like a very crunchy topping, spread mixed topping on a glass plate and **Micro on High 2 Minutes.** Let cool. Crumble and sprinkle over cooked yams.

CREAMY YAM CASSEROLE

Utensils: 6-1/2 x 8-1/2 flat oblong casserole
Time: 15 minutes
Servings: 6

**1 can (28 oz.) yams, drained
    and mashed (reserve
    liquid)
1/2 cup brown sugar
1/4 teaspoon salt
1/4 cup oleo or butter, melted
1 teaspoon vanilla
2 eggs, slightly beaten
1 cup pecans, chopped
1/8 cup yam juice
1 cup mini-marshmallows
1/4 cup evaporated milk**

1. In oblong casserole, mix all in-
    gredients except marshmallows.
    Micro on **High 5 Minutes,** then on
    70% Power 8 Minutes. Stick in
    marshmallows and Micro on **High
    about 2 Minutes.**

NOTE: All ingredients may be doubled if large casserole is needed. If
    so, Micro on **High 8 Minutes** then on **70% Power 12 Minutes.**

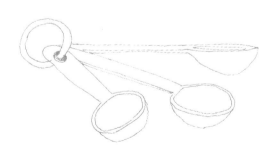

ZUCCHINI PROVOLONE

Utensils: 1-3/4 to 2 quart Corning dish
6" x 8" flat casserole
Time: 26 minutes
Servings: 6

2 tablespoons oleo
1 cup onion, chopped

1. In 1-3/4 to 2 quart dish, put oleo and onion. Micro on **High 5 Minutes.**

2 pounds (4 or 5) zucchini,
    peeled and sliced (4 cups)
2 cans (10 oz.) whole tomatoes,
    drained thoroughly and
    mashed
1 teaspoon salt
1/4 teaspoon cayenne pepper
1/4 teaspoon black pepper;
— dash garlic powder
1/2 teaspoon Italian seasoning

2. Add zucchini, tomatoes, salt, pepper, garlic powder and Italian seasoning. Micro on **High 18 Minutes, Covered** with lid. Stir once or twice. Drain off excess liquid.

1/3 cup Italian bread crumbs
1 tablespoon Parmesan cheese
1 package (6 oz.) sliced
    Provolone cheese

3. Stir in 1/3 cup bread crumbs and Parmesan cheese. In 6" by 8" casserole put half of tomato-zucchini mixture. Layer with half of Provolone cheese. Repeat with tomato mixture, then cheese.

1/4 cup Italian bread crumbs

4. Top with 1/4 cup bread crumbs. Micro on **High 3 Minutes.**

Rice
Jambalaya
Pasta
Grits
Roux

RICE
Microwave Rice 136
Mushroom Rice 137
Spanish Rice 138
JAMBALAYA
Creole Jambalaya 139
Creole Jambalaya - Package Prepared 140
PASTA
Spaghetti, Noodles, Etc. 140
GRITS
Grits 141
ROUX
Roux 141, 142

"Personal efficiency is creative self-management. It is not getting ahead of others, but getting ahead of yourself."

MICROWAVE RICE

Utensils: 2-3 quart dish and lid
Time: 22 minutes
Servings: 4-5

1 cup long grain rice
2 cups water
— dash of salt

1. In 2 or 3 quart dish, put water and salt. Micro on **High About 3 Minutes,** or until water is hot. Add rice. **Cover** with lid or plastic wrap. Micro on **50% Power** for **11 Minutes.** Stir. Re-cover and Micro on **50% Power** for **11 Minutes.** Let stand about 10 minutes. **(22 Minutes at 50% Power)**

FOR:
1-1/2 cups rice
3 cups water
— dash of salt

2. Micro Water until hot. Add rice. Cover and Micro on **50% Power** for **25-27 Minutes.** Stir halfway through cooking. Re-cover and continue cooking. Let stand about 10 minutes.

FOR:
2 cups rice
4 cups water
— dash of salt

3. Micro water until hot. Add rice. Cover and Micro on **50% Power** for **30-32 Minutes.** Stir halfway of cooking time. Re-cover and continue cooking. Let stand about 10 minutes.

NOTE: If you prefer a less moist rice, use 1 cup of rice to 1-2/3 cups of water and use same cooking times.

MUSHROOM RICE

Utensils: 2-1/2 to 3 quart dish
Time: 36 minutes
Servings: 6

1/2 pound fresh mushrooms, washed and cut in pieces, or 2 cans (4 oz.) mushroom pieces, drained
6 tablespoons oleo

1. In 2-1/2 to 3 quart dish, put mushrooms and oleo. Micro on **High 8 Minutes, Uncovered.**

1 can (10 oz.) onion soup plus juice from mushrooms and water to make 2 cups liquid

2. Add onion soup, juice from mushrooms and water. Micro on **High 3 Minutes, Uncovered.**

1 cup uncooked long grain rice

3. Add rice. Micro on **50% Power 25 Minutes, Covered** with glass lid or plastic wrap. Stir rice after cooking 12 minutes. Let stand 10 minutes.

NOTE: If canned mushrooms are used, omit Step 1. Add mushrooms to Step 2.

NOTE: Make certain you use 2 cups liquid.

SPANISH RICE

Utensils: 2-1/2 quart deep dish
Time: 33 minutes
Servings: 6

2 tablespoons oleo
1/2 cup onion, chopped

1. In 2-1/2 quart dish, put oleo and onion. Micro on **High 3 Minutes, Uncovered.**

1/3 cup green onions, chopped
1/4 cup green pepper, chopped

2. Add green onions and green pepper. Micro on **High 3 Minutes, Uncovered.**

1/2 pound smoked or hot
**   sausage, cut in pieces**
1 large can (12 oz.) V-8 juice
4 ounces water

3. Add sausage, V-8 juice and water. Micro on **High** about **3 Minutes,** until liquid is hot.

3 drops Worcestershire sauce
1 teaspoon parsley flakes
**   or fresh parsley**
— dash garlic powder
1 bay leaf
1/4 teaspoon cayenne pepper
1/2 teaspoon salt
1 cup raw rice

4. Add Worcestershire sauce, parsley, garlic powder, bay leaf, pepper, salt and rice. Stir. Cover with lid and Micro on **50% Power 12 Minutes.** Stir. Re-cover and Micro on **50% Power 12 More Minutes.** Let stand 10 minutes before serving.

CREOLE JAMBALAYA

Utensils: 3 quart deep dish
Time: 35 minutes
Servings: 6

1 tablespoon oil
1/2 cup onion, chopped

1. In 3 quart dish, put oil and onion. Micro on **High 4 Minutes.**

1/2 cup green onion, chopped
1/4 cup green pepper, chopped

2. Add green onions and green pepper. Micro on **High 3 Minutes.**

2 cups water
2 chicken bouillon cubes
1/2 teaspoon parsley flakes
1/2 teaspoon salt
1/2 teaspoon hot sauce
1 teaspoon Worcestershire
sauce
— dash garlic powder
1 teaspoon Kitchen Bouquet
pepper to taste

3. Add water, chicken cubes, parsley, salt, hot sauce, Worcestershire sauce, garlic powder, Kitchen Bouquet and pepper. Micro on **High** for about **3 or 4 Minutes** or until water starts to boil.

1 cup long grain rice
1 cup desired meat or seafood
(See Note)

4. Add rice and meat or seafood. Stir and cover with lid or plastic wrap (preferably with lid). Micro on **50% Power 12 Minutes.** Stir rice and Micro on **50% Power 12 Minutes More, Covered.** Let stand about 8-10 minutes.

NOTE: Sausage, ham or cooked chicken (chopped), or raw shrimp may be used.

NOTE: To increase recipe, increase amount of ingredients 1½ times and add **5 Minutes** cooking time.

CREOLE JAMBALAYA
PACKAGE PREPARED MIX

Utensils: 3 quart dish and cover
Time: 25 minutes
Servings: 4-6

**2-1/2 cups water or amount
called for on package**

1. In 3 quart dish, put water and Micro on **High 3 Minutes,** until water is very hot or boiling.

**1 package Creole Jambalaya
Mix (7.9 oz.)
1 cup sausage or ham,
chopped**

2. Add jambalaya mix and sausage. Stir. Cover with lid or plastic wrap, preferably a lid. Micro on **50% Power 11 Minutes,** stir. Re-cover and Micro on **50% Power 11 Minutes.** Let stand about 7-10 minutes.

SPAGHETTI, NOODLES, ECT.
(Pasta)

Utensils: 3 quart dish
Time: 15 minutes
Servings: 5-6

**1-1/2 quarts hot water
1 package (8 oz.) spaghetti,
noodles, etc.
1 teaspoon salt
1/2 teaspoon oil**

1. In 3 quart dish, put water, oil and salt. Bring to a boil. Add spaghetti. Micro on **High 15 Minutes** or until tender. Stir while cooking, (uncovered).

NOTE: If a larger package of pasta is used, then add more water and cooking time.

140

GRITS

Utensils: 2 quart dish
Time: 8 minutes
Servings: 3

1/2 cup grits
2 cups water
1/2 teaspoon salt
2 tablespoons butter or oleo

1. In 2 quart dish, put grits, water, salt and butter. Micro on **High 8 Minutes, Covered** with wax paper to prevent splatter. If started with hot water, time will be slightly lessened. Stir once or twice during cooking.

ROUX

A thick, rich, mysterious golden-brown sauce used for gumbos, stews, sauces and etouffees.

It is basically flour browned in butter, oil, or animal fat, to make gravy base for most Cajun dishes. The roux was normally a long and difficult process, but thanks to modern technology, we now have the miracle of the Microwave Oven, which makes the roux simple and even fun.

The directions for the roux in this book are based on an oven of 650 wattage. If your **Oven Wattage** is **Less Than 650,** you may have to **Add A Minute Or So** of cooking time. If your **Oven Is More Than 650,** you may have to **Subtract A Minute Or So** of cooking time.

Utensil:

You may use a **4 Cup Glass Measuring Cup, or Any Pyrex Glass or Corning Dish.** (Never plastic.) You may use the glass container that you will cook your stews or gravies in, but remember, **The Larger The Container Used, The Longer It Will Take To Make The Roux.** You have the option of using the same container to soil less dishes and take longer to cook the roux; or use a smaller container and take less time for roux and transfer roux into larger container to make stews, gravies, etc. (Larger the container, the longer the cooking time. Smaller the container, the shorter the cooking time.)

The following directions are for 3 different size rouxs, for whatever size your recipe calls for.

141

ROUX

1/4 cup oil **1/4 cup flour**	1. In 4 cup glass measuring cup or other utensil, mix oil and flour. Micro on **High 4-5 Minutes, Uncovered.** Just as the roux begins to turn a light brown, stir it since it will then begin to darken quickly and may burn. Continue cooking until it reaches a golden or nutty brown color. Stir again once or twice. Add chopped onion, green onion, green pepper and parsley in the amount called for in each recipe Saute' these vegetables for the amount of time called for in each individual recipe. (Time depends on the amount of vegetables used.)
1/2 cup oil **1/2 cup flour**	1. Directions same as above, except time is **5-6 Minutes.**
2/3 cup oil **2/3 cup flour**	1. Directions same as above, except time is **7-9 Minutes.**

NOTE: You may make a large amount of roux at once (omitting the vegetables) and freeze or store in the refrigerator. When using frozen or cold roux, you may add a few drops of oil to soften when reheating.

142

Eggs
Sauces
Corn Bread

EGGS

Hints on Eggs 146
Crawfish Omelet 147
Bologna N' Eggs for Breakfast 147
Eggs for Brunch 148
Creamy Cheese Scrambled Eggs 148
Eggs Poached in Cheese Sauce 149
Filled Omelet 150
    Cream Cheese Filling 150
    Hot Crab Filling 150
    Cheese Filling 150
    Bacon - Sour Cream Filling 151
    Ground Beef Filling 151
Red Hot Eggs 152
Fried Eggs 153
Poached Eggs 153

SAUCES

White Sauce 154
Cheese Sauce 154

CORN BREAD

Corn Bread From A Mix 155
Country Corn Bread 155

"The art of achievement is the art of making life — your life."

EGGS

Eggs are considered a delicate food; therefore, they are sensitive to microwave energy. The amount of time needed to cook eggs depend on several things:

1. **The Temperature of the Egg.**
2. **The Size of the Egg.**
3. **Whether the Egg is Cooked Whole or Scrambled or Mixed in Foods.**
4. **Whether the Recipe Calls for Water, Sugar or Fat.**

1. When cooking an egg whole, always puncture the yolk several times to prevent bursting.

2. Always cover eggs to prevent splatter (use casserole lids, plastic wrap, wax paper or paper towels).

3. Stir scrambled eggs once or twice for even cooking.

4. Since cooking continues after removed from oven, it is important not to overcook and to allow standing time. Because of the high fat content of the yolk, it will cook faster than the white; therefore, **Covering** and **Standing Time** are important. I prefer to cover with a glass lid while cooking to keep moist.

5. Do not cook eggs in shells. They will burst.

CRAWFISH OMELET

Utensils: 2-3 quart dish
Time: 17 minutes
Servings: 6-8

3 tablespoons butter
1/2 cup sliced mushrooms,
    drained or (4 oz. can)

1. In 2-3 quart dish, put butter and mushrooms. Micro on **High 2 Minutes.**

1/2 cup green onions, chopped
1-1/2 cups of crawfish tails

2. Add green onions and crawfish tails. Micro on **High 6 Minutes.**

6 eggs, beaten
1/2 teaspoon salt
1/8 teaspoon cayenne pepper

3. Mix eggs, salt and pepper. Pour over crawfish. Micro on **High 9-10 Minutes, Covered** with lid or plastic wrap. Center will not be set. Let stand 5 minutes. Stir once or twice during cooking.

NOTE: If oven does not have turntable, rotate dish twice during cooking.

BOLOGNA N' EGGS FOR BREAKFAST

Utensils: Custard cups
Time: 1-1/2 minutes
Servings: 1 or more

Bologna slices

1. Heat bologna between paper towels about 1/2 minute. (1 slice) Put slice of bologna in custard cup. Break egg over bologna. Pierce yolk.

cream (pet)

2. Top each with 1 teaspoon cream. Cover with plastic wrap. Micro on **70% Power 1 to 1-1/2 Minutes,** until firm as desired.

NOTE: For 2 eggs: 1-1/2 to 1-3/4 minutes.
          For 4 eggs: 2 to 2-1/4 minutes.

147

EGGS FOR BRUNCH

Utensils: 1 quart Corning dish
Time: 7 minutes
Servings: 4

2 tablespoons oleo
4 slices ham

1. In 1 quart dish, melt oleo, Add ham slices. Micro on **High 2 Minutes.** Remove ham slices from dish.

4 eggs, beaten
1/4 cup milk
1 tablespoon chives
1/4 teaspoon salt
— dash pepper
2 English muffins, split
    and toasted
4 slices any type cheese

2. To oleo in dish, add eggs, milk, chives, salt and pepper. Cover with lid. Micro on **70% Power 4 to 4-1/2 Minutes.** Stir after 3 minutes of cooking. Let stand 3 minutes. Top each muffin half with ham slice, then eggs, then a slice of cheese. Micro on **High 1 Minute.**

NOTE: Poached eggs may be used instead of scrambled in this recipe. (See poached eggs.)

CREAMY CHEESE SCRAMBLED EGGS

Utensils: 1 quart Corning dish and lid
Time: 5 minutes
Servings: 4-6

4 eggs
1/4 cup pet cream
1/4 teaspoon salt
— dash pepper
1/3 cup Cheddar cheese,
    grated
2 tablespoons oleo

1. In 1 quart Corning dish, mix all ingredients. Micro on **70% Power 5 Minutes, Covered.** Stir after 2 minutes and after 4 minutes. Let stand 3-4 minutes, covered.

EGGS POACHED IN CHEESE SAUCE

Utensils: 1 quart Corning shallow dish
Time: 10 minutes
Servings: 4

2 tablespoons oleo
3 tablespoons onion, chopped

1. In 1 quart dish, put oleo and onion. Micro on **High 2 Minutes.**

1 can (10-3/4 oz.) cream of
    celery soup
2/3 cup milk
1 cup Cheddar cheese, grated

2. Add soup, milk and cheese. Micro on **High 4 Minutes,** until mixture boils and cheese melts.

4 eggs
2 English muffins, split,
    toasted or slice bread,
    toasted

3. Carefully drop eggs into cheese mixture. Puncture egg yolks 2 or 3 times with toothpick to prevent bursting. Cover with lid. Micro on **High** about **4 Minutes,** or until eggs are as firm as desired. Spoon eggs and sauce onto English muffins or toast. Garnish with paprika and parsley flakes. Serve hot.

FILLED OMELET

Utensils: 8" pie dish
Time: 6 minutes
Servings: 1

3 eggs
2 tablespoons evaporated milk
2 tablespoons oleo
salt and pepper to taste

1. In 8" pie dish, put oleo. Micro until melted. In small dish, beat eggs, milk and salt and pepper. Pour into pie dish. Cover with glass lid or plastic wrap. Micro on **70% Power 6 Minutes.** Let stand 2 minutes, covered. Fill with favorite filling.

CREAM CHEESE FILLING

1 package (3 oz.) cream cheese
3 tablespoons sour cream
   (optional)
1 teaspoon chives

1. Mix all ingredients. Spread on omelet. Fold over. Micro on **High 30 Seconds.** Serve warm.

HOT CRAB FILLING

2 tablespoons oleo
1 teaspoon green onion,
   chopped
1 teaspoon parsley, chopped
3 tablespoons cream cheese
2 tablespoons sour cream
1/2 teaspoon lemon juice
1/4 cup crabmeat
salt and pepper to taste

1. In small dish, put oleo, onion and parsley. Micro on **High 1 Minute.** Add cream cheese, sour cream, lemon juice, crab meat, salt and pepper. Micro on **High 1 Minute.** Spread over omelet. Fold over. Serve warm.

CHEESE FILLING

1/2 cup any type cheese,
   grated

1. One minute before omelet is finished cooking, sprinkle with cheese. Return to oven. Cover and cook 1 more minute. Let stand 2 minutes. Fold omelet over in half. Serve warm.

BACON SOUR CREAM FILLING

**3 slices bacon, cooked and
    crumbled**
**1 teaspoon green onion,
    chopped, or 1 teaspoon
    chives**
3 tablespoons sour cream
salt and pepper to taste

1. Mix all ingredients and spread on
   omelet. Fold omelet in half. Serve
   warm.

GROUND BEEF FILLING

1/2 pound ground beef
1/4 cup onion
3 tablespoons oleo

1. In small bowl, put ground beef,
   onion and oleo. Micro on **High 5
   Minutes.**

1/2 cup tomato sauce

2. Add tomato sauce. Micro on **High
   5 Minutes, Covered** with lid or
   plastic wrap.

**1/2 cup any type cheese,
    grated**

3. Spread tomato-beef mixture on
   omelet. Sprinkle with cheese.
   Micro on **High 30 Seconds.** Fold
   omelet in half. Serve warm.

RED HOT EGGS

Utensils: 1 quart Corning flat dish
            1 small dish
Time: 19 minutes
Servings: 4

4 eggs
1-1/3 cups water

1. In 1 quart Corning dish put water. Micro on **High** until boiling (about 3 minutes). Drop eggs carefully into boiling water. Pierce yolks 2 or 3 times with tooth pick to prevent yolks from bursting. Cover with lid. Micro on **High 2-3 Minutes,** until as firm as desired. Remove eggs from dish and set aside. Wash and dry dish.

3 slices bacon
1/2 cup onion, chopped

2. In same 1 quart dish put bacon. Micro on **High** about **3 Minutes,** until crisp. Remove bacon and crumble and set aside. Discard all but 2 tablespoons bacon oil. Add onion to bacon oil. Micro on **High 2 Minutes.**

1 can (10 oz.) Ro-Tel tomatoes
**   and chilies, drained and**
**   mashed**
salt to taste

3. Add mashed tomatoes and salt. Micro on **High 5 Minutes.** Arrange eggs on top of tomatoes.

1 tablespoon oleo
1 tablespoon flour
1/2 cup milk
1/2 to 2/3 cup Cheddar cheese,
**   grated**
1/2 cup Italian bread crumbs

4. In small dish, put oleo. Micro on **High** until melted. Add flour. Stir. Add milk slowly, stirring. Stir in cheese. Micro on **High 1 Minute.** Stir once or twice during cooking to prevent lumping. Pour cheese sauce over eggs. Sprinkle with crumbled bacon. Sprinkle with bread crumbs. Micro on **High 1 Minute, Uncovered.**

NOTE: Regular canned tomatoes may be used in the place of Ro-Tel. If so, add pepper to taste.

FRIED EGG

Utensils: 10" Browning Skillet
Time: 45 seconds to 3-1/2 minutes

1 egg
2 tablespoons oleo

1. Put oleo in skillet. Micro on **High 2-1/2 Minutes.** Add eggs. Puncture egg yolk once or twice with toothpick to prevent bursting. Cover with lid. Micro on **70% Power 1 Minute.** Let stand covered 3 minutes.

2 eggs
2 tablespoons oleo

Time: 1-1/2 Minutes

3 eggs
3 tablespoons oleo

Time: 2-1/2 to 3 Minutes

4 eggs
3 tablespoons oleo

Time: 3 to 3-1/2 Minutes

POACHED EGGS

Utensils: 1 quart Corning shallow dish
Time: 6 minutes
Servings: 4

4 eggs
1-1/3 cups water
1 teaspoon vinegar

1.   In 1 quart Corning dish, put water. Micro on **High** until boiling (about 3 minutes). Add vinegar. Carefully drop in eggs. Puncture yolks 2 or 3 times with toothpick to prevent bursting. Cover with lid. Micro on **High 2-3 Minutes,** until desired firmness is reached. Remove eggs from water. Serve as desired.

NOTE: For 1 or 2 eggs, use small custard cup or bowl for each egg. Use 1/4 cup water, dash of vinegar and salt in each cup. Let water boil. Add egg and cover with plastic wrap. For 1 egg, Micro on **High 45 Seconds,** let stand 1 minute. For 2 eggs, Micro on **High 1 Minute-45 Seconds,** let stand 2 minutes.

SAUCE

WHITE SAUCE

Utensils: 4 cup glass measuring cup
Time: 3 minutes
Servings: 6

2 tablespoons oleo
2 tablespoons flour
1/2 teaspoon salt
1/2 teaspoon mustard

1.   In 4 cup measure, melt oleo. Add flour, salt and mustard.

1 cup of milk

2.   Add milk gradually. Micro on **High 3 Minutes,** stirring. Remove from oven.

2 egg yolks, beaten

3.   Stir in egg yolks slowly.

NOTE: For variety 2 hard boiled eggs can be grated into sauce.

CHEESE SAUCE

Utensils: 4 cup glass measuring cup
Time: 4 minutes
Servings: 6

2 tablespoons oleo
2 tablespoons flour
1/2 teaspoon salt
1/2 teaspoon mustard

1.   In 4 cup measure, melt oleo. Add flour, salt and mustard.

1 cup milk

2.   Add milk gradually. Micro on **High 3 Minutes,** stirring.

2 egg yolks, beaten

3.   Add egg yolks slowly.

1 cup Cheddar cheese, grated

4.   Add cheese and Micro on **High 1 Minute.**

CORN BREAD FROM A MIX

Utensils: Microwave pie dish or glass pie dish
Medium mixing bowl or food processor
Time: 7-9 minutes
Servings: 8

1 package (8-1/2 oz.) corn bread mix

1. In mixing bowl or food processor, mix corn bread according to package instructions. Pour into pan. Micro on **70% Power 7-9 Minutes,** until a tooth pick inserted in center comes out clean. Cover with foil and let stand 5 minutes.

COUNTRY CORN BREAD

Utensils: Microwave pie dish or glass pie dish
Medium mixing bowl or food processor
Time: 8 minutes
Servings: 8

1 cup flour
1 cup white cornmeal
1/4 cup sugar
1 teaspoon baking powder
1 teaspoon baking soda
3/4 teaspoon salt
1 egg
1 cup milk
3 tablespoons oleo
1/2 teaspoon vanilla

1. In mixing bowl or food processor, mix all ingredients until well blended. Pour into pie dish. Micro on **70% Power 8-9 Minutes,** until toothpick inserted in center comes out clean. Cover with foil and let stand 5 minutes.

Salads

SALADS

Cherry Pineapple Salad 158
Chicken Salad 159
French Potato Salad 160
Potato Spinach Salad 161
Taco Salad 162
Tomato Aspic Salad 163
Wilted Spinach Salad 164

"If you can imagine it, you can achieve it."

"A woman practices the art of adventure when she is unafraid of new ideas, new theories and new philosophies."

CHERRY PINEAPPLE SALAD

Utensils: 3 quart mixing bowl
　　　　　Mold
Time: 3 minutes
Servings: 8

1 can (16-1/2 oz.) black cherries, drained
1 can (15-1/2 oz.) crushed pineapple, drained
2 boxes (3 oz.) cherry gelatin

1. In 3 quart bowl, put cherry and pineapple juices. Micro on **High 3 Minutes.** Add gelatin and stir until dissolved.

2 (7-1/2 oz.) cokes or 13 ounces

2. Stir in coke. Refrigerate until slightly thickened.

1 cup miniature marshmallows
1 cup pecans, chopped (optional)
1 (8 oz.) package cream cheese

3. Fold in, thoroughly, cherries, pineapple, marshmallows, pecans and cream cheese (chopped in small chips). Pour into mold. Refrigerate until firm. Invert on platter.

CHICKEN SALAD

Utensils: 3 quart deep dish
            Large mixing bowl
Time: 30 minutes
Servings: 6-8

1 chicken (2-1/2 to 3 pounds), cut
2-1/2 cups hot water

1. In 3 quart dish, put chicken and water. Micro on **High 30 Minutes, Covered** with lid or plastic wrap. Remove chicken. Reserve broth. Grind chicken in grinder or food processor.

5 small pickles
5 boiled eggs
1 stalk celery

2. Grind pickles, eggs and celery. Add to chicken.

1/2 cup chicken broth
1-1/4 teaspoons salt
1/2 teaspoon cayenne pepper
1/4 teaspoon black pepper
1/2 cup mayonnaise
1/3 cup onion, chopped
**   very fine**
— dash of garlic powder

3. Add chicken broth, salt, pepper, mayonnaise, onion and garlic powder. Mix all ingredients thoroughly. Serve on lettuce leaf or make sandwiches.

FRENCH POTATO SALAD

Utensils: Medium salad bowl
            Small mixing bowl
Time: 15 minutes
Servings: 6

5 medium potatoes

1. (See baked potatoes.) Place potatoes on paper towel and Micro on **High 15-20 Minutes,** until tender. Wrap in foil and let stand 10 minutes. Chop and put in salad bowl.

4 eggs, boiled or poached hard, chopped
6 tablespoons mayonnaise
2 medium dill pickles, chopped
2 teaspoons parsley flakes
2 teaspoons dried minced onions
1 teaspoon chives (optional)
1/2 teaspoon mustard (dry or other)
3 teaspoons olive oil
3 teaspoons cayenne pepper
— dash black pepper
1 teaspoon salt
paprika

2. In small bowl, mix chopped eggs, mayonnaise, pickles, parsley, onions, chives, mustard, olive oil, pepper and salt. Add to potatoes and mix well. Sprinkle with paprika. Garnish with olives.

160

POTATO SPINACH SALAD

Utensils: Two 2-quart dishes
Dinner plate
Large salad bowl
Time: 32 minutes
Servings: 6-8

5 small or medium potatoes

1. See baked potatoes or wash and pierce potato skins. Micro on **High about 3-4 Minutes** per potato, or until tender. Slice into very thick slices. Put in 2 quart dish.

1 carton (8 oz.) fresh mushrooms

2. Wash mushrooms. Cut in halves. Drain and dry with paper towels. Put in 2 quart bowl. Micro on **High 8 Minutes.** Drain. Add to potatoes.

1 medium onion, sliced
1 large tomato, cut
1 bottle (8 oz.) Italian salad dressing

3. Add to potatoes: onion, tomato and salad dressing. Marinate 3 hours or overnight.

4 slices bacon
1 package (10 oz.) fresh spinach

4. Place bacon on paper towels on dinner plate. Micro on **High 4-5 Minutes,** until crisp. Crumble. In large salad bowl, put bacon and spinach. Add marinated mixture. Mix thoroughly. Serve immediately.

TACO SALAD

Utensils: 1-1/2 quart dish
Small mixing bowl
Large salad bowl
Time: 7 minutes
Servings: 8-10

1 pound lean ground beef
2 tablespoons Onion Soup Mix (packaged)

1. In 1-1/2 quart dish, put ground beef and onion soup mix. Mash with potato masher to separate. Micro on **High 7 Minutes, Uncovered.** Stir once or twice during cooking. Mash with potato masher once during cooking. Drain off liquid. May use colander. Set aside.

1 package (1.25 oz.) Sour Cream Mix

2. In small mixing bowl, put sour cream mix, and mix according to directions on package. Set aside.

1 medium head of lettuce, chopped
1 cup Cheddar cheese, grated
— dash of garlic
salt and pepper to taste
2 or 3 tomatoes, chopped
1 small avocado, chopped (optional)
1-1/2 to 2 cups tortilla chips, broken into small pieces

3. In large salad bowl, put ground beef, lettuce, cheese, garlic, salt, pepper, tomatoes, avocado and tortilla chips. Mix in sour cream mix. Toss. Serve immediately.

NOTE: 1 carton (8 oz.) sour cream may be substituted for package of sour cream mix.

TOMATO ASPIC SALAD

Utensils: 2-1/2 quart bowl
Time: 5 minutes
Servings: 8

**2 packages (3 oz.) lemon
    flavored Jell-O
3 cans (6 oz.) V-8 juice
3/4 cup tomato juice
20 drops hot sauce
1/2 teaspoon Worcestershire
    sauce
1 teaspoon salt
1 cup celery, chopped
1 to 2 pounds boiled shrimp,
    chopped, or 1 large can
    of shrimp, drained**

1. In 2-1/2 quart bowl, put V-8 juice and tomato juice. Micro on **High 5 Minutes.** Add Jell-o. Stir until completely dissolved. Add hot sauce, Worcestershire sauce, salt, celery and shrimp. Pour into small mold. Chill until congealed. Turn out on lettuce leaf. Serve with crackers.

NOTE: Two envelopes of unflavored gelatin may be used in place of Jell-o. If so, then add 2 tablespoons lemon juice.

WILTED SPINACH SALAD

Utensils: Large salad bowl
Small casserole dish
3 quart deep dish
Time: 16 minutes
Servings: 6

1 (one pound) package fresh spinach

1. Wash spinach. Drain and dry with paper towels. Set aside.

6 slices bacon
1/2 cup green onions, chopped

2. In small casserole, Micro bacon on **High 6 Minutes,** until crisp. Remove bacon and set aside. Add green onions. Micro on **High 2-3 Minutes.**

1 pound package (16 oz.) fresh mushrooms, washed, drained, and halved

3. In 3 quart dish, put above bacon drippings and onions. Add mushrooms. Micro on **High 5 Minutes,** until partly sauteed.

4 tablespoons wine vinegar
2 tablespoons lemon juice
2 teaspoons sugar
1-1/2 teaspoons salt
1/4 teaspoon black pepper
1/4 teaspoon mustard

4. Combine wine vinegar, lemon juice, sugar, salt, black pepper and mustard. Add **Crumbled** bacon bits. Add this mixture to the above mushrooms in 3 quart dish. Micro on **High 3 Minutes.** Place spinach in large salad bowl. Pour Hot mixture over spinach and mix until wilted. Serve hot.

NOTE: For variety you may add Parmesan cheese and 2 hard cooked eggs, chopped.

Cakes - Frostings
Pies - Cookies
Desserts - Candy

CAKES

Pastry Hints 169, 170
Banana Nut Cake 171
Carrot Pineapple Cake 172
Choco-Cheese Cake 173
Chocolate Caramel Cake 174
Chocolate Fudge Layer Cake 175
Cupcakes or Muffins 176
Fruit Cocktail Bundt Cake 177
Mississippi Mud Cake 178
Packaged Cake Mixes 179
Packaged Snacking Cakes 180
Pineapple Cream Cheese Coffee Cake 181
Rum Cake 182
Strawberry Shortcake 183

FROSTINGS

Chocolate Fudge Frosting 184
Chocolate Frosting/Bundt Cake 184
Chocolate Sour-Cream Frosting 185
Dark Chocolate Frosting 185
Fluffy White Frosting 186
Cream Cheese Frosting 186

PIES

Caramel Apple Pie 187
Cherry Creme Pie 188
Chocolate Raisin Pie 189
Choco-Vanilla Dream Pie 190
Coconut Creme Pie 191
Lemon Pineapple Pie 191
Watergate Pie 192
Cookie Crust 193
Frozen Pie Crust 193
Pie Crust 194
Graham Crumb Crust 194

COOKIES
Candy Bar Cookies 195, 196
Magic Cookie Bars....................................... 196
German Pecan Slices 197
DESSERTS
Apple Crunch Bread Pudding 198
Banana Bread Pudding.................................. 199
Brownies 199
Cherry Crunch Dessert................................. 200
Cinnamon Roll Breakfast Ring 200
Crunchy Pumpkin Squares 201
French Custard 202
French Toast 202
Hawaiian Pineapple Banana Creme Dessert or Pie 203
Pecan Filled Baked Pears 204
Sherried Fruit.. 204
Wine Gelatin Dessert................................... 205
CANDY
Candy Hints 206
Chocolate Covered Strawberries........................ 207
Chocolate Drops.. 208
Creamy Pralines 209
Heavenly Hash Candy................................... 210
Million Dollar Fudge 211
Passion Pralines 212
Peanut Brittle.. 213
Pecan Crunch 214
2 Minute Fudge 214

PASTRY

1. An excellent dish for mixing cake batter is the **8 Cup Measuring Cup** or utility dish or use food processor.

2. **A Round Cake Dish** produces a **More Evenly Cooked Cake** than a square.

3. If baking a slab cake or 7" x 11", or 9" x 13", put a small round dish or cup in center of cake pan before pouring in batter.

4. Prepare cake dish by putting **Wax Paper at Bottom of Dish.**

5. When mixing cake mixes for microwave ovens **Do Not Beat As Long** as box directions call for. Mix **Only Half Amount Of Time,** so you won't beat the air out. If using a food processor to mix, mix only 1/4 amount of time called for.

6. For **Layer Cakes** always **Use The Exact Amount Of Liquid Called For.** Do not decrease liquid.

7. One box of cake mix makes approximately 4 to 5 cups of batter. **Put 1/2 of Batter Into Pan** each time of cooking.

8. **Cook** only **One Layer** of cake **At The Time.**

9. Most layer and bundt cakes should be **Baked at 70% Power.**

10. **Snack Cake Mixes** can be baked on **High.**

11. The recipes in this book were tested in an oven which had a turntable; therefore, cakes and pies needed no turning. If your oven does not have a turntable, your **Cake or Pie Should Be Turned At Least Twice During Cooking Time.**

12. Cakes will not Brown, but most cakes are iced so that does not make any difference.

13. Microwave baked cakes will not fall when oven door is opened or closed.

14. **Cakes Are Done As Soon As Cake Leaves Sides Of Pan.**

PASTRY

15. If center of cakes (bundt, layer or slabs) are still moist when removed from oven, **Cover With Foil And Let Stand 7 Minutes.** If cake leaves sides of pan but center is still very under-cooked, **Add 1 Minute** at the time on **70% Power** until center is cooked.

16. Pie crust should be cooked before filling with fruit or custard or any other fillings.

17. When making cookie dough, divide batches after being mixed, according to the number of cups of flour used. If you mix a cookie dough recipe which calls for 2 cups of flour, divide mixed dough into 2 batches; if recipe calls for 3 cups of flour, divide mixed dough into 3 batches. Roll out each batch separately. Cut into cookie shapes desired and cook the whole batch at once on **High** for **4 Minutes.** (1 cup flour — 4 minutes cooking time on **High**.) (See No. 18)

18. **IMPORTANT:**
    Timing according to **Oven Wattage** is very important when cooking cakes or any pastries. Timing in most recipe books use 650 wattage as a guide for cooking.

If Your Oven Wattage Is:

LESS THAN 650 WATTAGE:
You should **Add A Little Cooking Time.**

OVER 650 AND UP TO 700 WATTAGE:
You should **Subtract A Little Cooking Time.**

700 WATTAGE AND OVER:
You should **Decrease The Power Level Setting** to the next lower setting than recipe calls for. (Example: If recipe calls for **70% Power,** use **60% Power** or **50% Power**.) Use the same time called for in the recipe.

BANANA NUT CAKE

Utensils: Medium size mixing bowl
           8″ microwave cake pan
Time: 16-17 minutes
Servings: 8

2 cups flour
1-1/3 cups sugar
2/3 teaspoon salt
2/3 teaspoon baking soda
2/3 teaspoon cinnamon

1. In medium bowl, stir flour, sugar, salt, baking soda and cinnamon.

2 eggs, beaten
2/3 cup oil
1-1/3 cups chopped bananas
1 teaspoon vanilla
2/3 cup pecans, chopped
1 can (8 oz.) crushed
    pineapple and juice

2. Stir in eggs, oil, bananas, vanilla, pecans and pineapple and juice. Pour half of batter into 8″ cake pan. Micro on **70% Power 7-8 Minutes,** as soon as batter begins to leave sides of pan. Let stand no more than 7 minutes. Turn on cake plate. Repeat for second layer.

NOTE: Frost with Fluffy White Frosting or Cream Cheese Frosting.

CAKE

CARROT-PINEAPPLE CAKE

Utensils: 3 quart mixing bowl
            9 or 10 cup bundt dish
Time: 13 minutes
Servings: 16 slices

1 box yellow cake mix
  (no pudding)
3 eggs
1/3 cup oil
1 (8 oz.) can crushed pineapple,
  drained, reserve juice
Juice of pineapple and enough
  water to measure 1/2 cup
2 teaspoons cinnamon
1/3 cup brown sugar
1-1/2 cups grated (very finely)
  carrots
1/2 cup raisins
1/2 cup pecans, chopped

1. In 3 quart dish, mix all ingredients. Pour into bundt dish. Micro on **70% Power 13 Minutes,** or just when cake begins to leave side of pan. Cake may still look uncooked. Cover cake tightly with foil or plastic wrap. Let stand about 7 minutes or until top looks done. Pass a knife around edge of cake to loosen any stuck particles. Invert on cake plate. Ice.

CREAM CHEESE ICING:

2 cups powdered sugar
2 (3 oz.) cream cheese
2 teaspoons vanilla
4 tablespoons oleo
1/3 cup raisins
1/3 cup pecans, chopped

2. Beat cream cheese, powdered sugar, vanilla and oleo. Add raisins and pecans. Spread over entire cake. If only a drizzled icing is preferred, cut icing recipe in half, micro 1 minute on high and drizzle over cake.

NOTE: Pineapple may be omitted. If it is omitted use 1/2 cup water for liquid.

NOTE: When baking a bundt cake you can tell when it is done when it just begins to leave the sides of the pan.

NOTE: If oven has no turntable, rotate dish twice during cooking.

CHOCO-CHEESE CAKE

Utensils: 1 quart mixing bowl
8" x 8" square baking dish
Small mixing bowl
Time: 9 minutes
Servings: 9

1 box (13 oz.) Moist and Easy Double Chocolate Chip Mix (Snacking Cake)
1 tablespoon oleo, melted

1. In 1 quart dish, mix cake mix according to directions on package. Add oleo. Pour 2/3 mixture in square dish. Set aside remainder of mixture.

2 (3 oz.) cream cheese
2 tablespoons oleo
1/4 cup sugar
4 tablespoons powdered sugar
2 tablespoons cornstarch
1 egg
1 teaspoon vanilla

2. Cream together cream cheese, oleo, sugar, powdered sugar and cornstarch. Beat in egg and vanilla. Spread cheese mixture over batter leaving the very center (the size of a small circle) free of cheese batter. (This helps the center cook more evenly.) Spread remainder of cake batter over cheese. Micro on **High 8 Minutes.** Cover with plastic wrap and **Add 1 Minute** at the time on **70% Power** until middle is firm. A toothpick inserted in center comes out clean. Top of cake may still seem moist. Let stand 5 minutes. Cool and frost.

FROSTING:

1 cup powdered sugar
2 tablespoons cocoa
2 tablespoons oleo
1 tablespoon milk
1/2 teaspoon vanilla

3. Put all ingredients in small bowl. Do not stir. Micro on **High About 1 Minute.** Stir until thick. Spread over cake.

CHOCOLATE CARAMEL CAKE

Utensils: 8″ round microwave or glass cake plate
Mixing bowl or food processor
2 small mixing bowls
Time: 17 minutes
Servings: 8

1 box (18 oz.) German chocolate cake mix

1. In mixing bowl or food processor, mix cake according to directions on package. Butter cake pan with oleo. Pour half of batter into pan. Micro on **70% Power 5-1/2 - 7 Minutes, Uncovered.** Let stand 5 minutes. Turn on cake plate. Pour remainder of batter into pan and repeat process. While cake is baking make filling.

CARAMEL FILLING:

42 light colored candy caramel candies (buy 14 oz. bag)
3 tablespoons evaporated milk
1/4 cup oleo
1-2/3 cups powdered sugar, sifted
1 cup pecans, chopped

2. In small bowl, put caramels and evaporated milk. Micro on **High 1-2 Minutes,** until melted. Stir in oleo, powdered sugar and chopped pecans. Spread half over first layer of cake. If icing is too thin, add more powdered sugar. Top with second layer. Frost top (not sides) with remainder of frosting (may drip down the sides).

CHOCOLATE FROSTING:

1/2 cup semi-sweet chocolate pieces
2 tablespoons evaporated milk
1 tablespoon oleo
1/2 teaspoon vanilla
1/2 cup powdered sugar, sifted

3. In small mixing bowl, put semi-sweet chocolate pieces and evaporated milk. Micro on **High 1 Minute,** until melted. Stir in oleo, vanilla and powdered sugar. Drizzle over caramel frosting.

NOTE: When cake leaves sides of pan it is done. If after cake starts to leave sides of pan the middle is completely uncooked right through middle, then add **1 Minute** at the time, of cooking time on **50% Power** until middle is done.

CHOCOLATE FUDGE LAYER CAKE

Utensils: 8 cup glass measuring cup
 8" round glass or microwave cake pan
Time: 12 minutes
Servings: 14-16

**1 package (17-18 oz.)
 chocolate cake mix**

1. In 8 cup measuring cup, prepare cake mix according to directions on package. Butter cake pan, then put a circle of wax paper over butter. Pour half of batter (about 2 or 2-1/2 cups) into pan. Micro on **70% Power 6-8 Minutes.** Cover cake with foil, plastic wrap or a plate for about 7 minutes. This will let the cake finish cooking. Pass a knife around edges of cake and invert on cake plate. Repeat with remainder of batter. Ice with Chocolate Fudge Icing.

(See Chocolate Fudge Icing)

NOTE: Just as cake starts to leave sides of pan, it is done. Sometimes the top will have the appearance of not being done, but covering after cooking will finish the cooking.

NOTE: If oven without turntable is used, turn cake at least twice during cooking.

NOTE: Another test for doneness is to insert a wooden pick into cake and it should come out clean.

NOTE: If after cake starts to leave sides of pan the middle of the cake is completely uncooked right through middle, then add **1 Minute** at the time, of cooking time on **50% Power** until middle is done.

CUPCAKES OR MUFFINS

Utensils: Muffin liners of cup cake pan
Time: 3-4 minutes per 6
Servings: as desired

**Cake batter or prepared
    muffin mix**

1.   Prepare batter as directed. Line
     cup cake pan with muffin liners.
     Spoon batter into muffin liners
     until half full. Micro on **70% Power
     Following Chart Below.**

70% POWER

6 cupcakes	3-4 minutes
4 cupcakes	2-1/2 minutes
2 cupcakes	1-1/2 minutes
1 cupcake	1 minute

FRUIT COCKTAIL BUNDT CAKE

Utensils: Bundt cake pan (buttered)
Medium mixing bowl or food processor
Time: 17 minutes
Servings: 16

1 package (18 oz.) Yellow cake mix.
1 can (16 oz.) fruit cockatil, drained, (reserve juice)
2 eggs
1/4 cup oil
1/2 cup brown sugar

1. In medium mixing bowl or food processor, mix for 1 minute the cake mix, reserved fruit juice, eggs and oil. Stir in fruit cocktail. Pour into buttered bundt pan. Sprinkle with brown sugar. Micro on 70% **Power 13 Minutes.** Remove from oven. Cover with foil for 7 minutes. Pass sharp knife around edges and inner circle. Turn over on cake plate. Frost.

FROSTING

1/2 cup sugar
1/2 cup evaporated milk
1/2 cup oleo
1/2 teaspoon vanilla
1/2 cup pecans, chopped
1/2 cup coconut (optional)

1. In small bowl, put all ingredients. Micro on **High 4-5 Minutes** until thick. Spread on top of cake.

MISSISSIPPI MUD CAKE

Utensils: 8″ x 8″ square dish or round microwave cake pan
Small dish
Time: 4-1/2 minutes
Servings: 9

1 box Stir N' Frost Chocolate Devil's Food Cake Mix (Betty Crocker)

1. Empty contents of package into square dish. Put required amount of water (2/3 cup). Stir until not lumpy. Micro on **High 4 Minutes, Covered** with a paper towel.

About 18 marshmallows
1/2 cup pecans, chopped (optional)

2. Top with marshmallows. Sprinkle with pecans. Micro on **High 30 Seconds.**

1 package Chocolate Frosting (included in package of cake mix)

3. Cut open package of frosting. Put contents in small dish. Micro a few seconds until melted. Drizzle over marshmallows.

NOTE: Stir N' Frost is a Snacking Cake.

NOTE: If oven does not have a turntable, turn cake once during cooking.

PACKAGED CAKE MIXES

Utensils: 8 cup glass measuring cup or mixing bowl
            8″ glass or microwave cake pan
Time: 8 minutes
Servings: 14-16

**1 package (17-18 oz.) cake mix
(any type)**

1. In 8 cup measuring cup or bowl, put cake mix. Mix according to directions on package. (Do not decrease liquid as some microwave books may say. It makes cake dry.) Butter cake pan then line with wax paper. Pour half of batter (about 2 or 2-1/2 cups) into pan. Micro on **70% for 5-1/2 - 7 Minutes.** When cake is done it begins to leave side of pan. Toothpick will come out clean when inserted in center of cake. Cover cake with foil, plastic wrap or plate for about 7 minutes. (This will complete the cooking process.) Invert on cake plate and repeat with remainder of cake batter.

NOTE: Top of cake may not look completely done before covering with foil and letting stand for 7 minutes.

NOTE: If oven without turntable is used, cake should be turned or rotated at least twice during cooking.

NOTE: If after cake starts to leave sides of pan the middle of the cake is completely uncooked through middle, then add **1 Minute** at the time of cooking time on **50% Power** until middle is done.

PACKAGED SNACKING CAKES

Utensils: 8″ x 8″ square dish
Time: 6-1/2 to 7-1/2 minutes
Servings: 6-8

Betty Crocker
    Stir N' Frost
Plus 1 tablespoon oil

1. Prepare mix according to directions on package. Add oil. Pour into 8″ x 8″ square dish. Micro on **High 6-1/2 Minutes.** Let stand 5 minutes covered with foil.

Duncan Hines
    Snacking Cake
1 tablespoon oil

1. Prepare mix according to directions on package. Add oil. Pour into 8″ x 8″ square dish. Micro on **High 7-1/2 Minutes.** Let stand 5 minutes covered with foil.

NOTE: If oven wattage is over 650, a little less time is needed.
If oven wattage is under 650, a little more time is added.

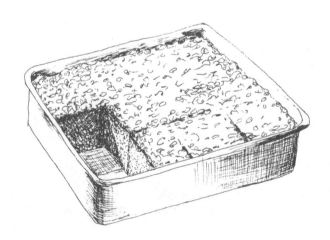

PINEAPPLE CREAM CHEESE COFFEE CAKE

Utensils: Medium mixing bowl or food processor
8″ round microwave cake plate
Glass plate
2 small bowls
Time: 7-1/2 minutes
Servings: 6-8

1 can (8 oz.) crushed pineapple, drained. (Reserve juice).
1/4 cup oleo
1/3 cup sugar
1 large egg
1 teaspoon vanilla
1-1/2 cups all purpose flour, sifted
1-1/2 teaspoons baking powder
1/4 teaspoon salt

1. In medium mixing bowl or processor, mix oleo, sugar, egg, and vanilla. Stir in pineapple juice, flour, baking powder and salt. Top with drained pineapple.

1 package (3 oz.) cream cheese
1 tablespoon sugar
2 teaspoons lemon juice

2. In small bowl, mix cream cheese, sugar and lemon juice. Spread over pineapple. Micro on **70% Power 7 Minutes.**

1/4 cup brown sugar
4 tablespoons flour
2 tablespoons oleo, room temperature
1/4 cup pecans, chopped

3. In small bowl, mix sugar, flour, oleo and pecans. Spread on plate. Micro on **High 2-1/2 Minutes.** Let cool. Crumble. Sprinkle over coffee cake.

RUM CAKE

Utensils: Medium mixing bowl or food processor
              Bundt cake pan
Time: 12 minutes
Servings: 16

1/2 cup pecans, chopped
1 package (17 oz.) yellow
    cake mix
1 package instant vanilla
    pudding
3 eggs
1/3 cup oil
3/4 cup water
1/2 cup rum

1. Butter bundt cake pan. Sprinkle pecans on bottom. Mix for 1 minute: the cake mix, pudding, eggs, oil, water and rum. Pour into bundt pan. Micro on **70% Power 11 Minutes.** Pierce top of cake thoroughly with two prong fork. Pour glaze over top. Cool for 15 minutes. Turn over on cake plate.

GLAZE:

1 stick butter (8 tablespoons)
1 cup sugar
1/4 cup water
1 ounce rum

1. In small mixing bowl, put butter, sugar and water. Micro on **High 1 Minute.** Add rum. Pour over cake.

STRAWBERRY SHORTCAKE

Utensils: Medium mixing bowl or food processor
Microwave cake dish
Medium bowl
Time: 15 minutes
Servings: 16

1 package (17 oz.) yellow cake mix

1. In medium bowl or food processor, mix cake mix according to package. Mix for 1 minute. Pour half of batter into cake dish. Micro on **70% Power 5-1/2 to 6 Minutes,** until cake leaves sides of dish. Cover with foil. Let stand 7 minutes. Turn over on cake plate. Repeat for remainder of batter. Turn second layer on a separate plate and serve as two short cakes or fill first layer with following strawberry filling and Cool Whip. Put second layer on top, then put more filling on second layer and top with more Cool Whip.

STRAWBERRY FILLING:

2 packages (10 oz.) frozen strawberries
2 tablespoons corn starch
1 tablespoon water
1 carton (12 oz.) Cool Whip

1. In medium dish, put strawberries, corn starch and water. Micro on **High 4 Minutes,** or until thick. Cool. Spread on layers and top with Cool Whip.

CHOCOLATE FUDGE FROSTING

Utensils: 2 quart dish
Time: 2 minutes

6 tablespoons cocoa
1 block (8 tablespoons) oleo
1/4 cup milk
1 box (1 pound) powdered
  confectioners sugar
  (sifted)
1/4 teaspoon salt

1. In 2 quart dish, put cocoa, oleo, milk, powdered sugar and salt. Do not stir. Micro on **High 2-3 Minutes,** until oleo is melted. Stir until starts to thicken.

1 teaspoon vanilla
1/2 cup nuts, chopped
  (optional)

2. Stir in vanilla and nuts. Stir until thick enough to spread. As you frost the cake, if icing gets too thick, add a little milk.

NOTE: Fills and frosts two 8″ layers.

NOTE: For a lighter chocolate icing use less cocoa.

CHOCOLATE FROSTING FOR BUNDT CAKE

Utensils: Small bowl
Time: 1 minute

1-1/2 tablespoons cocoa
1 tablespoon water
2 tablespoons oleo
1 cup powdered sugar

1. In small bowl, put all ingredients. Micro on **High 1 Minute.** Stir and drizzle over cake. If too thick, add a little more water.

184

CHOCOLATE SOUR-CREAM FROSTING

Utensils: Medium size bowl
Time: 3-4 minutes
Serving: Frosts and fills one 2-layer cake

1 package (12 oz.) semi-sweet chocolate pieces	1. In medium size bowl, put chocolate pieces. Micro on **50% Power 3-4 Minutes** until melted. Stir once or twice during cooking. Cool.
1 cup sour cream **— dash of salt**	2. With mixer, beat in sour cream and salt until creamy and of spreading consistency. Fill and frost cake.

DARK CHOCOLATE FROSTING

Utensils: Medium size bowl
Time: 3-4 minutes
Serving: Frosts and fills one 2-layer cake

1 package (6 oz.) semi-sweet chocolate pieces **1/2 cup evaporated milk** **1 cup butter or oleo**	1. In medium size bowl, put chocolate pieces, milk and oleo. Micro on **50% Power** until chocolate is melted. Stir once or twice.
2-1/2 cups confectioners' sugar, sifted	2. With beater, beat in sugar until spreading consistency. May have to cool slightly to thicken before spreading.

185

FLUFFY WHITE FROSTING

Utensils: Small mixing bowl
Time: 1 minute

1 egg white
3/4 cup sugar
— dash of salt
1 teaspoon vanilla
— dash of cream of tartar

1. In small mixing bowl, mix egg white, sugar, salt, vanilla and cream of tartar.

1/4 cup BOILING water
5 tablespoons powdered sugar

2. Add boiling water and beat until very thick and fluffy. Beat in powdered sugar.

CREAM CHEESE FROSTING

Utensils: Small mixing bowl

1 package (8 oz.) cream cheese
1 cup oleo
1 box (16 oz.) powdered sugar, sifted
1 teaspoon vanilla

1. Beat cream cheese and oleo. Add powdered sugar and vanilla. Beat well.

186

CARAMEL APPLE PIE

Utensils: 8" or 9" pie dish
           3 quart bowl
           2 small bowls
Time: 15 minutes
Servings: 6-8

1 frozen pie crust, defrosted

1. Put pie crust in glass pie dish. Micro on **High 4 Minutes.**

4 large apples, peeled and cut
1/2 cup white sugar
1/3 cup brown sugar
1/4 cup flour
1/2 teaspoon cinnamon
3 tablespoons oleo
1/4 cup evaporated milk

2. In 3 quart dish, put apples, white sugar, brown sugar, flour, cinnamon, oleo and evaporated milk. Micro on **High 6 Minutes,** stirring. Pour into pie crust.

1 small egg
1 package (3 oz.) cream cheese
1/4 cup sugar
10 caramel candy squares
1 tablespoon evaporated milk

3. Beat together egg, cream cheese and sugar. Drizzle in strips over apples. In small bowl, put caramels and evaporated milk. Micro on **High about 1 Minute,** until melted. Drizzle caramel mixture in between cream cheese mixture.

1/4 cup pecans,
**   chopped**

4. Sprinkle with pecans. Micro on **High 4 Minutes.**

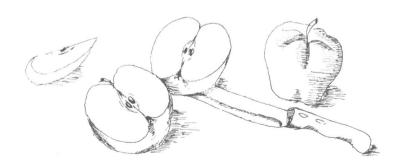

187

CHERRY CREME PIE

Utensils: 2 quart dish
              8" or 9" pie dish
              Small bowl and 1-1/2 to 2 quart bowl for topping
Time: 13-1/2 minutes
Servings: 8

1 frozen pie shell

1. Let pie shell partially thaw. Transfer shell into pie dish. Micro on **High 4 Minutes.**

FILLING:

1 cup evaporated milk
1 cup water
1/2 cup whole milk
1 teaspoon vanilla

2. In 2 quart dish, put evaporated milk, water, whole milk and vanilla.

4 tablespoons cornstarch
2/3 cup sugar

3. In small bowl, mix together cornstarch and sugar. Add to milk. Micro on **High 7-8 Minutes,** until very thick, stirring at intervals while cooking. Let cool. Pour into pie shell.

TOPPING:

1 (1 pound) can pitted dark
    sweet cherries
1/4 cup sugar
2 tablespoons cornstarch

4. Drain cherries. Reserve juice. In 2 quart bowl, mix sugar and cornstarch. Stir in cherry juice. Micro on **High about 2-1/2 Minutes,** until thick. Add cherries and stir. Cool and spoon over custard. Serve cold.

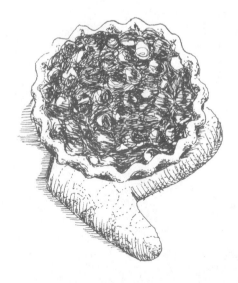

188

CHOCOLATE RAISIN PIE

Utensils: 8″ or 9″ pie dish
4 small bowls
Time: 9 minutes
Servings: 8

1 - 8″ or 9″ frozen pie shell, slightly defrosted

1. Put pie shell in glass pie dish. Micro on **High 4 Minutes.**

1/4 cup sugar
1 envelope unflavored gelatin
1 cup milk
1/2 cup semi-sweet chocolate pieces
2 egg yolks, slightly beaten
1 tablespoon instant coffee crystals (optional)
1/8 teaspoon salt

2. In small bowl, mix sugar and gelatin. Stir in milk, chocolate and coffee crystals. Micro on **High 3 Minutes,** stirring once or twice. Remove from oven. Stir in beaten egg yolks and salt.

*1 cup raisins (see note)
1/4 cup rum

3. In small bowl put raisins and rum. Micro on **High 2 Minutes.** Add to above chocolate mixture. Chill until partially set.

2 egg whites, room temperature
1/4 cup granulated sugar

4. In small bowl, beat egg whites. Add sugar gradually, beating after each addition. Fold into gelatin mixture. Chill until mixture mounds.

1 cup whipping cream
1/4 cup powdered sugar

5. In small bowl, beat whipping cream until forms soft peaks. Add powdered sugar. Beat together until well blended. **Fold** carefully into chocolate-egg white mixture. Do not beat or mix. Spoon into cooked pie shell. Chill until firm.

NOTE: Pecans may be substituted for the raisins in this pie. If so, omit the cooking in step 3, just add rum and pecans to chocolate mixture.

189

CHOCO-VANILLA DREAM PIE

Utensils: 8" or 9" pie plate
2 quart dish
Small dish
Time: 6-1/2 minutes
Servings: 6-8

2 cups chocolate sugar cookies, crushed (may use blender)
1/3 cup oleo

1. In pie plate, melt oleo. Add cookie crumbs. Mix and press to form shell. Micro on **High 3 Minutes.**

30 large marshmallows or 4 cups marshmallows
1 can (13 oz.) evaporated milk
1 envelope unflavored gelatin

2. In 2 quart dish, put marshmallows, evaporated milk and gelatin. Stir. Micro on **High 3 Minutes.** Cool in refrigerator until starting to gel. Beat until fluffy.

1/2 pint whipping cream, whipped or 1 small container (9 oz.) Cool Whip
2 tablespoons creme de menth or 1 teaspoon peppermint extract

3. Mix in whipped cream or Cool Whip. Add creme de menth or extract. Pour over pie crust.

1/2 cup powdered sugar
2 teaspoons oleo
1-1/2 tablespoons cocoa
2 teaspoons water

4. In small dish, put sugar, oleo, cocoa and water. Micro on **High 30 Seconds.** Drizzle pie with chocolate. Place in refrigerator and chill until firm.

COCONUT CREAM PIE

Utensils: 8″ or 9″ glass pie dish
Blender or food processor
Time: 12 minutes
Servings: 8

4 eggs
1/2 cup soft oleo
3/4 cup sugar
1 teaspoon vanilla
1/2 cup biscuit mix
1-1/2 cups milk
1 cup grated coconut

1. In blender or food processor, mix all ingredients except coconut. Pour into greased pie dish. Sprinkle with coconut. Micro on **70% Power 12 Minutes,** until firm. Cover and let stand 10 minutes, until set.

LEMON PINEAPPLE PIE

Utensils: 2 quart bowl
Time: 11 minutes
Servings: 8

1 box lemon pie filling mix
    (requires cooking)
1/4 cup water
1/2 cup sugar
2 egg yolks
1-1/2 cups water
1 can (8-1/4 oz.) crushed
    pineapple

1. In 2 quart bowl, put pudding. Add 1/4 cup of water and sugar. Add egg yolks and 1-1/2 cups water and pineapple and juice. Micro on **High 6-7 Minutes.** Cool completely. Stir once or twice during cooking.

1 9-inch pie shell (baked)
    (see frozen pie shell)

2. Pour into baked pie shell. Top with cool whip or meringue. If using meringue, use favorite meringue recipe, spread on pie and bake in conventional oven according to recipe directions.

WATERGATE PIE

Utensils: Small bowl
              Large mixing bowl
              9" glass pie dish
Time: 5 minutes
Servings: 8

1 - 9" frozen pie shell or cookie crust

1. See frozen pie shell or cookie crust.

1 envelope unflavored gelatin
1/2 cup cold water
1 can (1 pound 4 oz.) crushed pineapple and juice

2. In small bowl, put water and sprinkle gelatin over water. Stir. Micro on **High 30 Seconds** or until dissolved. Stir in pineapple and juice. Chill until it begins to gel.

1 carton (8 oz.) Cool Whip
2-1/4 cups miniature marshmallows
1 package instant Pistachio pudding mix
1 cup pecans, chopped

3. In large mixing bowl, mix well: Cool Whip, marshmallows, pudding mix and pecans. Stir in pineapple mixture thoroughly. Spoon into pie shell and chill until firm.

COOKIE CRUST

Utensils: Small mixing bowl
9″ glass pie dish
Time: 7 minutes
Serving: 1 pie shell

1-1/4 cups flour
1/2 cup oleo, softened, but
**   not melted**
1/4 cup sugar
1 egg, slightly beaten
1 teaspoon vanilla

1. In small bowl, mix all ingredients. Shape around pie dish to form crust. Micro on **70% Power 7 Minutes.**

FROZEN PIE CRUST

Utensils: 8″ or 9″ pie dish
Time: 4 minutes
Servings: 8

1 frozen pie crust,
**   slightly defrosted**

1. Transfer crust into glass pie dish. Micro on **High 4 Minutes.** Or: Micro on **70% Power 4 Minutes,** then on **High 1 Minute.**

NOTE: If pie crust is thick you may have to add **30 Seconds to 1 Minute** cooking time on **High.**

PIE CRUST

Utensils: Glass pie plate
Time: 4-5 minutes
Servings: 8

**1-1/4 cups unsifted all-
    purpose flour
1/2 teaspoon salt
1/2 cup oleo
2-1/2 to 3 tablespoons
    cold water**

1. Mix flour and salt in medium size
    mixing bowl. Cut in oleo with
    pastry blender until resembles
    coarse meal. Add water. Mix until
    dough clings together and forms
    ball. Chill. Roll out on lightly
    floured wax paper. Line pie plate.
    Micro on **High 4-5 Minutes** until
    crisp.

GRAHAM CRUMB CRUST

Utensils: Glass pie dish
Time: 2 minutes
Servings: 8

**1 cup fine graham cracker
    crumbs
3 tablespoons sugar
3 or 4 tablespoons oleo,
    softened**

1. Mix all ingredients. Press into pie
    dish. Micro on **High 2 Minutes.**

NOTE: You may use chocolate wafers or gingersnap crumbs for variety.

CANDY BAR COOKIES
(You Will Love These)

Utensils: Medium size mixing bowl for flour
2 small bowls
Time: 9 minutes
Servings: 36 cookies

3/4 cup oleo
3/4 cup powdered sugar
2 tablespoons evaporated milk
1 teaspoon vanilla
1/4 teaspoon salt
2 cups all purpose flour,
sifted

1. In medium mixing bowl, cream oleo. Add powdered sugar gradually. Cream well. Add evaporated milk, vanilla and salt. Mix well. Stir in flour until mixed thoroughly. Divide dough in half. To each half add 3 tablespoons flour. Stir. Put one half of dough between two pieces of wax paper. Roll out dough to about a 12" x 8" rectangle. Cut into about 3" x 1-1/2" rectangles or 2" squares. Use glass bottom of oven as a cookie sheet. Butter bottom of oven. Place the complete first batch of cookies in circles in oven. If you oven wattage is 650, Micro on **High 5 Minutes.** Let cool slightly. Remove with spatula. Set aside. If your oven is between 650-700, Micro on **High 4 Minutes.** If your oven is 700 or over wattage, Micro on **90% Power 5 Minutes.** Repeat with second batch of cookies.

CARAMEL FILLING:

1/2 pound or 28 caramel
candies
1/4 cup evaporated milk
1/4 cup oleo
1 cup powdered sugar, sifted
1 cup pecans, chopped

1. In small bowl, put caramels and evaporated milk. Micro on **High 2 Minutes.** Stir. Add oleo, powdered sugar and pecans. Stir well. Put a small scoop of caramel mixture on each cookie.

CHOCOLATE FILLING:

1 package (6 oz.) semi-sweet chocolate pieces
1/3 cup evaporated milk
2 tablespoons oleo
1 teaspoon vanilla
1/2 cup powdered sugar, sifted

1. In small bowl, put chocolate pieces and evaporated milk. Micro on **High 2 Minutes.** Stir in oleo, vanilla and powdered sugar. Mix well. Put a small amount over caramel on each cookie. You may top each cookie with a pecan half.

NOTE: When making cookies, divide your dough into separate batches. Use 1 cup of flour per batch. Example: If your recipe called for 2 cups of flour, divide your mixed dough into 2 batches; if the recipe called for 3 cups of flour, divide your mixed dough into 3 batches. Cook each batch between 4-5 minutes. (1 cup of flour — 4-5 minutes of cooking).

MAGIC COOKIE BARS

Utensils: Medium size mixing bowl
            7" x 11" oblong casserole dish
Time: 8-9 minutes
Servings: 36 bars

1/2 cup oleo, melted
1-1/2 cups graham cracker crumbs
1 cup pecans, chopped
1 cup (6 oz. package) semi-sweet chocolate pieces
1 can (15 oz.) sweetened condensed milk

1. In medium size mixing bowl, mix all ingredients. Spread into a 7" x 11" oblong dish. Micro on **High 8-9 Minutes,** until a wooden toothpick comes out clean when inserted in center. Cover with foil and let stand 8-10 minutes. Cool slightly and cut into squares.

GERMAN PECAN SLICES

Utensils: 2 small mixing bowls
7" x 11" oblong flat casserole dish
Time: 16 minutes
Servings: 16 squares

1-1/4 cups flour
1/2 cup oleo, melted
1/4 cup sugar
1 egg, slightly beaten
1 teaspoon vanilla

1. Mix well in small bowl: flour, oleo, sugar, egg and vanilla. Pat down in 7" x 11" oblong dish. Micro on **70% Power 7 Minutes.**

1-1/2 cups brown sugar
2 tablespoons flour
1/2 teaspoon baking powder
2 eggs, slightly beaten
1 teaspoon vanilla
1-1/2 cups pecans, chopped

2. In small bowl, mix sugar, flour and baking powder. Add eggs, vanilla and pecans. Spread over baked dough. Micro on **70% Power 9 Minutes.** Spread with icing. Let cool. Cut in squares.

ICING

1 cup powdered sugar
1-1/2 tablespoons lemon juice

1. Mix together powdered sugar and lemon juice. Micro on **High 30 Seconds.** Spread over baked pecan mixture.

197

APPLE CRUNCH BREAD PUDDING

Utensils: Microwave cake pan or 9" pie dish
Time: 8 minutes
Servings: 6

2 eggs, slightly beaten
1 cup sugar
2 cups milk
1 tablespoon vanilla
6 slices bread, broken up
2 medium apples, chopped
2/3 cup raisins (optional)

1. In cake pan or pie dish, mix all ingredients. Micro on **High 5 Minutes.** Stir. Sprinkle on topping. Micro on **High 3 Minutes.** Let stand 10 minutes.

TOPPING:

2 tablespoons plus
**   1/2 teaspoon flour**
1/2 cup dark brown sugar
1/2 cup pecans, chopped
**   (optional)**
1-1/2 tablespoons oleo, melted

2. Mix all ingredients and sprinkle on pudding.

NOTE: If no topping is desired, add 1/4 cup sugar to pudding and still stir after 5 minutes.

NOTE: For plain bread pudding, omit apples and follow above directions.

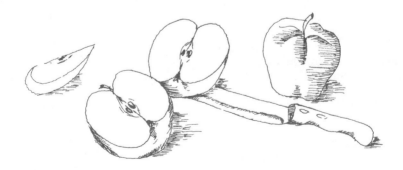

BANANA BREAD CUSTARD

Utensils: Microwave cake pan or 9" glass pie dish
Time: 8 minutes
Servings: 6

2 eggs, slightly beaten
1 cup sugar
2-1/4 cups milk
1 tablespoon vanilla
6 slices bread, broken up
2 bananas, cut
2/3 cup raisins (optional)

1. In cake pan or pie dish, mix all ingredients. Micro on **High 5 Minutes.** Stir. Micro on **High 3 Minutes.** Let stand 7-10 minutes. Top with custard.

CUSTARD TOPPING:
Utensils: 2 quart dish
Time: 6 minutes

1/3 cup sugar
1/4 cup cornstarch
2-1/3 cups milk
1/2 teaspoon salt
3 egg yolks, beaten
1 teaspoon vanilla
1 teaspoon oleo

1. In 2 quart dish, mix sugar and cornstarch. Slowly stir in milk. Add salt and egg yolks. Stir well. Micro on **High 6-7 Minutes,** until very thick. Stir during cooking. Stir well after cooking to remove any lumps. Add vanilla and oleo.

BROWNIES

Utensils: 9" cake dish
                 Medium mixing bowl
Time: 9-10 minutes
Servings: 10

1 package (15 oz.) brownie
mix

1. In medium mixing bowl, mix according to package directions. Pour into greased cake dish. Micro on **70% Power 9-10 Minutes, Uncovered.** Cooked when wooden toothpick in center comes out clean.

199

CHERRY CRUNCH DESSERT

Utensils: 8" x 8" square dish or 9" glass pie dish
Time: 16 minutes
Servings: 6-8

1 can (21 oz.) cherry pie filling
1 box (9 oz.) yellow cake mix
4 tablespoons oleo
1/2 cup pecans, chopped

1. Spread pie filling mix in square or round dish. Mix together cake mix and oleo until crumbly. Add pecans. Spread over pie filling. Micro on **High 16-17 Minutes.** Serve with whipped cream, Cool Whip or ice cream.

CINNAMON ROLL BREAKFAST RING

Utensils: Microwave cake pan or 8" or 9" pie dish
Time: 4-1/2 minutes
Servings: 8

1/4 cup butter or oleo
1/2 cup brown sugar
1 package (8) refrigerator
cinnamon rolls

1. Micro oleo in small dish until melted. Dip rolls in oleo, then in brown sugar. Arrange in pie dish. Sprinkle remainder of brown sugar over rolls and also any remaining oleo.

1/2 cup raisins
1/2 cup pecans, chopped
(optional)

2. Sprinkle with raisins and nuts. Put small plastic container of icing on saucer and Micro a few seconds until soft. Drizzle over rolls. Micro on **70% Power 4-1/2 Minutes.** Let stand 3 minutes.

NOTE: For a quickie you may omit raisins and pecans or even icing. Kids love it any way. A terrific quick breakfast.

200

CRUNCHY PUMPKIN SQUARES

Utensils: 2 medium size mixing bowls
Small bowl
7" x 11" oblong dish
Glass plate
Time: 25 minutes
Servings: 16

1 package (18 oz.) yellow cake mix (reserve 1 cup)
1/2 cup oleo
1 egg, beaten

1. In medium size mixing bowl, mix cake mix (less 1 cup), oleo and egg. Pat evenly into 7" by 11" oblong dish. Micro on **70% Power 6 Minutes,** then on **50% Power 1 Minute.** Set aside.

1/4 cup oleo, melted
1 cup cake mix
1/2 cup sugar
1/2 cup pecans, chopped

2. In small bowl, melt oleo. Add cake mix, sugar and pecans. Spread evenly on glass plate. Micro on **High 3 Minutes.** Let cool and crumble into a crunch.

1 can (18 oz.) pumpkin pie filling
1/3 cup milk
1/4 cup brown sugar
1 teaspoon cinnamon

3. In medium size bowl, put pie filling, milk, sugar and cinnamon. Micro on **70% Power 15 Minutes.** Stir once or twice during cooking. Spread over cake. Sprinkle with crunch. Slightly pat crunch down on pumpkin. Cool. Cut in squares.

FRENCH CUSTARD

Utensils: 2 quart dish
Time: 6 minutes
Servings: 6

1/3 cup sugar
1/4 cup cornstarch
1-1/3 cups milk
1/2 teaspoon salt
3 egg yoks, beaten
1 teaspoon vanilla

1. In 2 quart dish, mix sugar and cornstarch. Slowly stir in milk. Add salt and egg yolks. Stir well. Micro on **High 5-6 Minutes,** until desired thickness is acquired. Stir during cooking. Add vanilla.

NOTE: This custard may be used for cream puffs. If so, add 1 tablespoon oleo after cooking.

FRENCH TOAST

Utensils: 10" browning skillet
          Flat dish
Time: 3 minutes
Servings: 12

4 eggs
1/2 cup pet cream
2/3 cup sugar
1 teaspoon vanilla
— dash cinnamon

1. In flat dish, mix eggs, cream, sugar, vanilla and cinnamon.

6 tablespoons oleo
12 slices bread

2. Put 2 tablespoons oleo in browning skillet and melt. Dip 4 slices of bread in egg mixture and lay in browning skillet. Micro on **High 1-1/2 Minutes.** Turn bread over. Micro on **High 1-1/2 Minutes** more.

HAWAIIAN PINEAPPLE BANANA CREME DESSERT (OR PIE)

Utensils: 8" or 9" pie plate or microwave cake pan
Small dish
Time: 8 minutes
Servings: 6-8

Baked 8" or 9" pie shell (see frozen pie shell or graham cracker crust) 3 tablespoons oleo, melted 1 tablespoon honey 1 can (8 oz.) crushed pineapple 1/4 teaspoon lemon juice 1/4 teaspoon cinnamon	1. In small dish, put oleo, honey, pineapple and juice, lemon juice and cinnamon.
3 teaspoons cornstarch 3 tablespoons cold water	2. Mix together cornstarch and water and add to pineapple mixture. Micro on **High 2 Minutes** or until mixture is thick.
5 bananas 1/4 cup pecans, chopped	3. Slice bananas in pie shell. Pour pineapple mixture over bananas. Sprinkle with pecans. Micro on **High 6 Minutes.**
1 (8 oz.) package cream cheese 1/2 cup powdered sugar 1 cup Cool Whip or 1 package Dream Whip mixed according to package. 1/4 cup pecans, chopped 1/2 cup coconut (optional)	4. Beat cream cheese. Add sugar. Mix in Cool Whip. Spoon over pineapple. Sprinkle with pecans and coconut.

NOTE: Can be used as a dessert by omitting pie shell. May also be spooned over ice cream, omitting cream cheese topping.

PECAN FILLED BAKED PEARS

Utensils: 8" x 8" square dish
            Small bowl
Time: 5 minutes
Servings: 6-8

1 large can (29 oz.) pears,
    drained
1/2 cup pecans, chopped
1 tablespoon evaporated milk
1/4 cup brown sugar
2 tablespoons oleo, melted
1/2 teaspoon vanilla
1/4 teaspoon cinnamon

1. In small bowl, mix all ingredients
    except pears. Put drained pears in
    square dish. Fill with pecan
    mixture. Micro on **High 5 Minutes.**

SHERRIED FRUIT

Utensils: 7" b 11" oblong casserole
            1-1/2 quart dish
Time: 13 minutes
Servings: 12

1 medium can (20 oz.) sliced
    pineapple, drained
1 can (16 oz.) peach halves,
    drained
1 jar (5 oz.) apple rings, drained
1 can (17 oz.) apricot halves,
    drained

1. In 7" by 11" oblong casserole,
    arrange fruit.

3 tablespoons flour
1/2 cup brown sugar
1 block (8 tablespoons) oleo
2/3 cup sherry
1/2 cup pecans, chopped
    (optional)

2. In 1-1/2 quart dish, put flour,
    brown sugar, oleo, sherry and
    pecans. Micro on **High about 3
    Minutes** or until thickened. Pour
    over fruit. Micro on **High 10
    Minutes.** Serve hot.

NOTE: This may be made with only two or three fruit instead of four.

204

WINE GELATIN DESSERT

Utensils: 2 or 2-1/2 quart bowl
Individual mold dessert dishes or 1 medium mold
Time: 4 minutes
Servings: 8

1 can (16 oz.) fruit cocktail, drained, reserve juice
juice of fruit cocktail plus enough water to equal 3 cups
2 envelopes unflavored gelatin
1 cup sugar
2/3 cup sweet red wine
1 tablespoon lemon juice

1. In 2 quart bowl, put fruit juice and water. Sprinkle gelatin over liquid. Stir. Micro on **High 2 Minutes.** Stir. Add sugar. Micro on **High 2 Minutes** to dissolve sugar. Add wine, lemon juice and fruit cocktail. Stir well. Chill until congealed. To serve, top with 2 scoops of vanilla ice cream.

205

CANDY

1. Candy is very easy to make in your microwave oven. Cooking occurs on all sides rather than just the bottom.

2. The **Dish** used should be **Two To Three Times As Large as the Volume of Candy** being cooked. An excellent dish for cooking candy is the 8 cup glass measuring cup or utility dish.

3. You may use a **Microwave** candy thermometer.

4. Do not make divinity when the humidity is high, it will not harden.

5. To test for candy temperature stages drop a little cooked mixture into a cup half-filled with cold water. (See Candy Chart.)

6. After cooking time for candy is complete, let stand 7-10 minutes without stirring. Then stir or beat slowly until it starts to thicken and starts to lose its gloss before pouring or dropping.

7. **Candy Temperature Chart:**

SOFT BALL 240°F Fudge Fondant	A small amount dropped into 1/2 cup of cold water forms a small soft ball that can be picked up with fingers but flattens.
FIRM BALL 244-248°F Caramels	When dropped in cold water retains its shape when removed from water.
HARD BALL 250-266°F Divinity, Nougat, Taffy, Caramel Popcorn	A small amount dropped in 1/2 cup cold water forms a firm ball and can be picked up.
SOFT CRACK 270-285°F Butterscotch Toffee Taffy	A small amount dropped in water sets into a brittle thread which will bend or break separate into threads, but not brittle.
HARD CRACK 290-310°F Brittle Glace'	A small amount dropped in water forms into a brittle thread which snaps without bending.

CHOCOLATE COVERED STRAWBERRIES

Utensils: 2 small bowls
Time: 2 minutes
Servings: 20-30

Fresh strawberries, small to medium size

1. Wash and stem berries. Drain and set aside.

1 block butter (8 tablespoons)

2. Let butter soften at room temperature.

1 tablespoon evaporated milk

3. Add cream.

1 box (16 oz.) powdered sugar, sifted

4. Stir in powdered sugar. Take a small amount of mixture in hand. Press in palm of hand. Place strawberry in center. Form a ball around berry.

1 pound unsweetened chocolate
1/4 block paraffin wax

5. In small bowl, put chocolate and wax. Micro until wax melts. Place berry on a two prong fork and dip into chocolate. Place on waxed paper. Let cool.

CHOCOLATE DROPS

Utensils: 8 cup measuring cup (glass)
Time: 11 minutes
Servings: 20-30

1 block oleo (8 tablespoons)
1 box Light Brown sugar
  (3 cups)
1 small can (5.33 oz.)
  evaporated milk
  room temperature
— dash salt
2-1/4 cups miniature
  marshmallows

1.   In 8 cup measuring cup, put oleo, sugar, evaporated milk, salt and marshmallows. Stir. Micro on **High 11 Minutes.** Stir 2 or 3 times during cooking.

1 package (6 oz.) semi-sweet
  chocolate pieces
  (see note)

2.   Add semi-sweet chocolate pieces and stir until melted.

1 teaspoon vanilla
1-1/2 cups pecans, chopped

3.   Add vanilla and pecans and stir just until mixed. Let mixture stand awhile, then **stir** slowly until it starts to thicken. Around the top of the bowl, mixture will start to harden a little. Drop by spoonful on foil or wax paper. Do not **beat** fudge.

NOTE: If possible, use Hershey's chocolate pieces. Nestles chocolate seems to take very long to dissolve.

CREAMY PRALINES

Utensils: 8 cup glass measuring cup
Time: 12 minutes
Servings: 20-30

**2/3 block oleo or butter
(6 tablespoons)
1 small can (5.33 oz.)
evaporated milk
2 cups Light Brown sugar
1-1/4 cups miniature marshmallows
— dash of salt**

1. In 8 cup measuring cup, put oleo, evaporated milk, brown sugar, marshmallows and salt. Mix. Micro on **High 13 Minutes,** stirring occasionally.

**1 teaspoon vanilla
1 cup pecans, chopped**

2. Stir in vanilla and pecans. Let mixture stand 10 minutes, then **stir** slowly until it starts to thicken. Around the top of the bowl, the mixture will start to harden. Drop by teaspoon on foil or wax paper. **Do Not Beat** mixture.

NOTE: In order for these pralines to harden they have to be stirred until they are beginning to get slightly hard in the bowl.

NOTE: For variety try MAPLE NUT PRALINES. To the above recipe add (after vanilla): a dash of nutmeg, a dash of cinnamon and 1/4 teaspoon maple flavoring.

HEAVENLY HASH CANDY

Utensils: 8 cup glass measuring cup
              7" x 11" oblong casserole
Time: 11 minutes
Servings: 20 pieces

**1 box (16 oz.) powdered
  confectioners sugar
4 tablespoons oleo
1 small can (5.33 oz.)
  evaporated milk
1 teaspoon cocoa
2-1/4 cups mini-marshmallows**

1. In 8 cup glass measuring cup, put confectioners sugar, oleo, evaporated milk, cocoa and marshmallows. Stir. Micro on **High 11 Minutes,** stirring once or twice.

**12 ounces of milk chocolate
  pieces
1 tablespoon vanilla
1½ cups pecans, chopped
3 teaspoons water**

2. Add milk chocolate pieces. Stir until melted. Add vanilla and pecans. Stir until starts to thicken. Add water. Pour ½ of mixture into a buttered 7" x 11" oblong dish.

**2 cups large marshmallows,
  cut in half**

3. Put marshmallows on top of chocolate mixture. Pour or spread remainder of chocolate mixture over marshmallows. Let cool. Cut in squares.

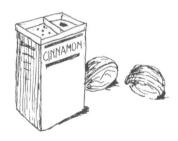

MILLION DOLLAR FUDGE

Utensils: 8 cup glass measuring cup or utility dish
7" x 11" oblong casserole dish
Time: 10 minutes
Servings: 35-40 pieces

3 cups sugar
8 tablespoons oleo or (1 block)
— dash of salt
2/3 cup evaporated milk
(1 small can 5.33 oz.)
2-1/4 cups mini-marshmallows

1. In 8 cup measuring cup, or bowl, put sugar, oleo, salt, evaporated milk and marshmallows. Stir. Micro on **High 10 Minutes.** Stir once or twice during cooking. If mixture begins to boil over during cooking, stop oven and let mixture settle down before restarting oven.

1 package (6 oz.) semi-sweet
chocolate pieces
1 package (6 oz.) milk
chocolate pieces

2. Add chocolate pieces and stir until melted.

1 teaspoon vanilla
1-1/2 cups pecans, chopped
(optional)

3. Stir in vanilla and pecans. Stir slowly until mixture begins to thicken. Pour into oblong dish. Let set and cut into squares.

NOTE: For a darker chocolate fudge, use 2 packages of semi-sweet chocolate and omit milk chocolate.

For a milk chocolate fudge, use 2 packages of milk chocolate pieces and omit semi-sweet chocolate pieces.

211

PASSION PRALINES

Utensils: 8 cup measuring cup (glass)
Time: 11 minutes
Servings: 20-30

**1 block butter or oleo
  (8 tablespoons)
1 box Dark Brown sugar
  (3 cups)
1 small can (5.33 oz.)
  evaporated milk, room
  temperature
— dash salt
2-1/4 cups miniature
  marshmallows**

1. In 8 cup measuring cup, put oleo, sugar, evaporated milk, salt and marshmallows. Stir. Micro on **High 11 Minutes.** Stir 2 or 3 times during cooking.

**1 package (6 oz.) semi-sweet
  chocolate pieces
  (see note)**

2. Add semi-sweet chocolate pieces and stir until melted.

**1 teaspoon vanilla
1-1/2 cups pecans, chopped**

3. Add vanilla and pecans and stir just until mixed. Let mixture stand a few minutes then **stir** slowly until it starts to thicken. Around the top of the bowl, mixture will start to harden a little. Drop by spoonful on foil or wax paper. (Do not **Beat** pralines.)

NOTE: If possible use Hersheys or Bakers chocolate. Nestles chocolate seems to take longer to dissolve.

NOTE: For an entirely different praline, try substituting Hersheys milk chocolate pieces in place of semi-sweet pieces.

PEANUT BRITTLE

Utensils: 8 cup glass measuring cup
　　　　　　Flexible cookie sheet
Time: 9 minutes
Servings: 20

1 cup granulated sugar **1/2 cup white corn syrup**	1.　In 8 cup measuring cup, put sugar and corn syrup. Micro on **High 4 Minutes.**
1 cup salted, roasted peanuts (Spanish peanuts are excellent)	2.　Add peanuts. Micro on **High 3-4 Minutes.**
1 teaspoon butter or oleo **1 teaspoon vanilla**	3.　Add butter and vanilla. Micro on **High 1 Minute.** Stir.
1 teaspoon baking soda	4.　Add baking soda and stir until foamy. Pour and spread mixture onto **Lightly Greased** cookie sheet. Cool and break into pieces.

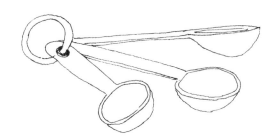

PECAN CRUNCH

Utensils: 8 cup glass measuring cup
Flexible cookie sheet
Time: 9 minutes
Servings: 20

1 cup granulated sugar
1/2 cup white corn syrup

1.   In 8 cup measuring cup, put sugar and corn syrup. Micro on **High 4 Minutes.**

1/8 teaspoon salt
1 cup pecan pieces

2.   Add salt and pecans. Micro on **High 3-4 Minutes.**

1 teaspoon butter or oleo
1 teaspoon vanilla

3.   Add butter and vanilla. Micro on **High 1 Minute.** Stir.

1 teaspoon baking soda

4.   Add baking soda and stir until foamy. Pour and spread mixture on to a **Lightly Greased** cookie sheet. Cool and break into pieces.

2 MINUTE FUDGE

Utensils: 8 cup glass measuring cup
7" by 11" oblong dish
Time: 2 minutes
Servings: 20

1 box (1 pound) powdered confectioners sugar, sifted
1/2 cup cocoa
1/4 cup milk
1/2 cup oleo

1.   In 8 cup measuring cup, put powdered sugar and cocoa. Add milk and oleo. Do not stir! Micro on **High 2-3 Minutes** until oleo is melted.

1 teaspoon vanilla
1/2 cup nuts, chopped (optional)

2.   Stir in vanilla and nuts. Stir until mixture starts to thicken. Spread in buttered dish. Refrigerate for about 15 minutes, or until firm. Cut into squares. Keep refrigerated.

EQUIVALENTS

LIQUID MEASURE VOLUME EQUIVALENTS

60 drops = 1 teaspoon

3 teaspoons = 1 tablespoon

2 tablespoons = 1 fluid ounce

4 tablespoons = ¼ cup

5-1/3 tablespoons = 1/3 cup

8 tablespoons = ½ cup or 4 ounces or
1 gill or 1 tea cup

16 tablespoons = 1 cup or 8 ounces

⅜ cup = ¼ cup plus 2 tablespoons

⅝ cup = ½ cup plus 2 tablespoons

⅞ cup = ¾ cup plus 2 tablespoons

1 cup = ½ pint or 8 ounces

2 cups = 1 pint or 16 ounces

1 quart = 2 pints or 64 tablespoons

1 gallon = 4 quarts

DRY MEASURE VOLUME EQUIVALENTS

2 cups = 1 pint

2 pints = 1 quart

4 quarts = 1 gallon

2 gallons or 8 quarts = 1 peck

4 pecks = 1 bushel

MISCELLANEOUS MEASURE EQUIVALENTS

A few grains = Less than ⅛ teaspoon

Pinch = As much as can be taken between
tip of finger and thumb

Speck = Less than ⅛ teaspoon

1 jigger = 2 ounces

1 minim = 1 drop

10 drops = dash

6 dashes = 1 teaspoon

8 teaspoons = 1 ounce

CHEESE MEASUREMENTS

1 pound American cheese = 4 cups grated

1 pound Cheddar cheese = 4 cups grated

4 ounces Cheddar cheese = 1 cup grated, sieved or chopped

1 pound Cottage cheese = 2 cups

½ pound Cottage cheese = 1 cup or 8 ounces

½ pound Cream cheese = 1 cup or 8 ounces

6 ounces Cream cheese = 12 tablespoons or ¾ cup

5 ounces Cheese spread = 8 tablespoons or ½ cup

BUTTER OR MARGARINE MEASUREMENTS

1 pound = 4 sticks or 2 cups

1 cup = 2 sticks

¼ cup = 4 tablespoons

½ cup = 8 tablespoons

½ cup = 1 stick

¼ cup = ½ stick

¾ cup = 12 tablespoons

1 cup = 16 tablespoons

APPROXIMATE INGREDIENT SUBSTITUTIONS AND EQUIVALENTS

1 teaspoon baking powder = ¼ teaspoon baking soda plus ½ cup buttermilk
                                = ¼ teaspoon baking soda plus ½ teaspoon cream
                                     of tartar
Leavening
   (per cup flour) = Use 1¼ teaspoon baking powder, or ¼ teaspoon soda
                          with 2 tablespoons vinegar
1 pound sifted flour = 4 cups
1 cup sifted all purpose flour = 1 cup plus 2 tablespoons sifted cake flour
1 cup sifted cake flour = ⅞ cup sifted all purpose flour
1 pound granulated sugar = 2 to 2¼ cups
1 teaspoon sugar = ¼ grain saccharin
                    = ⅛ teaspoon non-caloric sweetner
1 pound confectioners sugar = 4 to 4½ cups
1¾ cups packed confectioners sugar = 1 cup granulated
1 pound brown sugar = 2¼ to 2½ cups
1 cup packed brown sugar = 1 cup granulated
1 cup honey = 1 to 1¼ cups sugar plus ¼ cup liquid
1 cup corn syrup = 1 cup sugar plus ¼ cup liquid
1 cup butter = 1 cup margarine
               = 14 tablespoons hydrogenated fat and ½ teaspoon salt
               = 14 tablespoons lard and ½ teaspoon salt
1 cup fresh milk = ½ cup evaporated milk plus ½ cup water
                  = ½ cup condensed milk plus ½ cup water (reduce sugar
                     in recipe)
                  = 4 teaspoons powdered whole milk plus 1 cup water
                  = 4 tablespoons powdered skim milk plus 2 teaspoons butter
                     plus 1 cup water
1 cup buttermilk or sour milk = 1 tablespoon vinegar or lemon juice plus
                                  enough sweet milk to make one cup (let stand 5
                                  minutes) or 1¾ teaspoon cream of tartar plus
                                  1 cup sweet milk.
1 cup yogurt = 1 cup buttermilk
1 cup coffee or light cream = 3 tablespoons butter and about ¾ cup milk
1 cup heavy cream = ½ cup butter and about ¾ cup milk
1 cup whipping cream = 2 cups or more after whipping
2 large eggs = 3 small eggs
1 ounce chocolate = 1 square or 3 tablespoons cocoa plus 1 teaspoon to
                  1 tablespoon fat (less for Dutch-type cocoa)
1 tablespoon flour = ½ tablespoon cornstarch or arrowroot, or 2 teaspoons
                     quick-cooking tapioca (as thickener)
1 tablespoon cornstarch = 2 tablespoons flour (as thickener)
1 tablespoon potato flour = 2 tablespoons flour (as thickener)
1 teaspoon lemon juice = ½ teaspoon vinegar
Herbs, ½ to 1½ teaspoon dried = 1 tablespoon fresh
2 tablespoons chopped green pepper = 1 tablespoon dried pepper flakes
1 teaspoon fresh herbs = 1/3 teaspoon dried

¼ cup onion = 1 tablespoon dried flakes or 1 teaspoon powder
⅛ teaspoon garlic powder = 1 small clove
1 tablespoon candied ginger, washed of sugar or 1 tablespoon raw ginger = ⅛
    teaspoon powdered ginger
1 tablespoon fresh horseradish = 2 tablespoons bottled
1 cup raw rice = approximately 3 cups cooked
1 cup uncooked macaroni = 2 to 2¼ cups cooked
1 cup uncooked noodles = 1¾ cups cooked
1 pound fresh mushrooms = 3 ounces dried or 6 ounces canned
15 pounds whole crawfish = 1 pound peeled tails
1 cup onion = 1 medium onion

METRIC CONVERSION CHART

1 tsp.	=	5 ml.
1 Tbl.	=	15 ml.
1 oz.	=	30 ml.
1/4 c.	=	59 ml.
1/3 c.	=	79 ml.
1/2 c.	=	119 ml.
1 c.	=	237 ml. or 0.24 l.
1 pt.	=	473 ml. or 0.47 l.
1 qt.	=	946 ml. or 0.95 l.
1 gal.	=	3785 ml. or 3.8 l.
1 liter	=	1000.0 ml.
1 oz. (dry)	=	28 grams
1 pound	=	454 grams or 0.45 kilograms
1 gram	=	0.035 ozs.
1 kilogram	=	2.2 pounds

HOW TO CONVERT:

From	To	Multiply By
tsp.	ml.	5
Tbsp.	ml.	15
1 oz.	ml.	30
cups	l.	0.24
pints	l.	0.47
quarts	l.	0.95
gallons	l.	3.8
pounds	kil.	0.45
ounces	grams	28
grams	ounces	0.035
kilograms	pounds	2.2
milliliters	ounces	0.03
liters	pints	2.1
liters	quarts	1.06
liters	gallons	0.26

GENERAL INDEX

APPETIZERS
Artichoke Balls 3
Bacon and Water Chestnut Appetizer 3
Baked Beef Dip 4
The Big Dipper 4
Cheese Rarebit 5
Dipsy Devil Dip 5
Hot Cheese Crackers... 6
Marinated Party Vegetables.. 6
Marinated Vegetables 7
Raw Vegetable Dip... 8
Crab Dip 9
Shrimp or Crab Dip I 10
Shrimp or Crab Dip II 10
Crawfish Dip.. 11

SOUPS
Cajun Oyster Soup... 14
Creamy Oyster Soup 15
Green Thumb Soup 16
Onion Soup 17
Vegetable Soup 18

GUMBOS
Chicken Okra Gumbo 19
Seafood Gumbo 20
Shrimp Okra Gumbo 21

MEATS AND MEAT DISHES
Hints on Cooking Meat.. 24
Preparing Convenience Meats 25
Meat Defrosting... 26
Barbecued Ribs... 27
Beef or Pork Roast.. 28
Brown Gravy for Roast 29
Beef Stew Country 30
Curried Shrimp or Ground Beef.................................... 31
Barbecued Sausage or Chicken Spaghetti 32
Fresh Sausage with/without Wine Sauce 33
Chili and Bean Enchilada Casserole............................... 34
Chili and Beans... 35
Cowboy Annie's Beer Chili 36
Hot Dog Chili... 37
Dirty Rice Dressing 38
French Oyster Dressing 39
Baked Ham 40
Hot Ham Sandwich 41
Ham and Cheese Meatloaf.. 42
Hamburgers 43
Lasagna 44
Lasagna II 44, 45
Mazetti 46
Barbecued Pork Chops 47
Breaded Pork Chops 48
Pork Chops in Brown Gravy 48
Stuffed Green Peppers 49

POULTRY
Poultry Hints 52
Poultry Defrosting 53
Poultry Roasting Chart 53
Roast Chicken 54
Roast Turkey 55
Cooked Chicken 56
Barbecued Chicken 56
Oven Crispy Chicken.. 57
Sweet and Sour Chicken 57
Chicken Enchilada Casserole 58
Chicken Stew... 59
Cream of Chicken Quiche 60
Golden Chicken Souffle 61
Herbed Chicken 62
Hot Chicken Salad Casserole 63
Mandarin Chicken 64
Ritzy Chicken.. 65
Italian Chicken Spaghetti Casserole................................ 66
No Tomato Chicken Spaghetti Casserole 67

SEAFOOD
Hints on Seafood 70
Defrosting Seafood 70
Seafood Cooking Chart 70

FISH
Baked Flounder with Crab Stuffing................................. 71
Catfish or Trout Broiled in Butter Sauce........................... 72
Red Fish or Trout Alexandra...................................... 73

SHRIMP
Barbecued Shrimp 74
Barbecued Shrimp La Sal and Sams 74
Italian Steamed Shrimp.. 75
Shrimp and Crab Stew 76
Shrimp Creole 77
Shrimp in Crabmeat Sauce 78
Shrimp Scampi 79

CRABS
Baked Crabmeat Casserole 80
Crabmeat Artichoke Au Gratin 81
Crabmeat Au Gratin... 82
Prize Winning Crabmeat Patties................................... 83

CRAWFISH
Crawfish Delicacy... 84
Crawfish Etouffee 85
Crawfish Rice Casserole... 86

OYSTERS
Oysters Bienville or Casserole 87
Oysters Broussard 88
Oysters Conrad 89
Herbed Oysters 90

SEAFOOD CASSEROLE
Tuna Mushroom Bake 91
Salmon in Tomato Sauce 92
Seafood Bake 93

VEGETABLES
Vegetable Hints 96
Vegetable Cooking Charts 96, 97, 98
Delicious Artichokes 99
Baked Beans 99
Holland and French Beets Combo 100
Broccoli Chicken Casserole 101
Broccoli Rice Casserole 102
Shrimp Broccoli Casserole 103
Beef and Cabbage Bake 104
Glorified Cabbage 105
Stuffed Cabbage Rolls 106
Cauliflower Au Gratin 107
Cauliflower La Bienville 108
Cauliflower Supreme 109
Corn and Tomato Creole 110
Corn on the Cob 110
Eggplant and Shrimp Casserole 111
Eggplant Parmesan 112
Cheesy Green Bean Casserole 113
Green Beans, French Style 114
Southern Field Peas 115
Tiny Green Peas, Southern Style 116
Baked Potatoes / Boiled / Sweet 117
Chili Potatoes 118
Smothered Potatoes, French Style 119
Italian Potatoes 120
Potatoes Anna 120
Pizza Potato Casserole 121
Potato Bake Casserole 122
Potatoes Au Gratin 123
Sour Cream Potato Casserole 124
Stuffed Potatoes A La New Orleans 125
Tuna Stuffed Potatoes 126
Creamed Spinach 127
Filled Acorn Squash/Pineapple or Cranberries 128
Summer Squash with Shrimp 129
Yam Praline Crunch 130
Creamy Yam Casserole 131
Zucchini Provolone 132

RICE
Microwave Rice 136
Mushroom Rice 137
Spanish Rice 138

JAMBALAYA
Creole Jambalaya 139
Creole Jambalaya - Package Prepared 140

PASTA
Spaghetti, Noodles, Etc. 140

GRITS
Grits 141

ROUX
Roux 141, 142

EGGS
Hints on Eggs 146
Crawfish Omelet 147
Bologna N' Eggs for Breakfast 147
Eggs for Brunch 148
Creamy Cheese Scrambled Eggs 148
Eggs Poached in Cheese Sauce 149
Filled Omelet 150
    Cream Cheese Filling 150
    Hot Crab Filling............................. 150
    Cheese Filling 150
    Bacon - Sour Cream Filling................. 151
    Ground Beef Filling 151
Red Hot Eggs...................................... 152
Fried Eggs.. 153
Poached Eggs 153

SAUCES
White Sauce 154
Cheese Sauce 154

CORN BREAD
Corn Bread From A Mix 155
Country Corn Bread 155

SALADS
Cherry Pineapple Salad 158
Chicken Salad 159
French Potato Salad 160
Potato Spinach Salad 161
Taco Salad 162
Tomato Aspic Salad............................... 163
Wilted Spinach Salad............................. 164

CAKES
Pastry Hints 169, 170
Banana Nut Cake 171
Carrott Pineapple Cake........................... 172
Choco-Cheese Cake 173
Chocolate Caramel Cake 174
Chocolate Fudge Layer Cake 175
Cupcakes or Muffins 176
Fruit Cocktail Bundt Cake 177
Mississippi Mud Cake 178
Packaged Cake Mixes 179
Packaged Snacking Cakes......................... 180
Pineapple Cream Cheese Coffee Cake 181
Rum Cake 182
Strawberry Shortcake 183

FROSTINGS
Chocolate Fudge Frosting 184

FROSTINGS *(continued)*

Chocolate Frosting/Bundt Cake.................................. 184
Chocolate Sour-Cream Frosting 185
Dark Chocolate Frosting 185
Fluffy White Frosting 186
Cream Cheese Frosting 186

PIES

Caramel Apple Pie 187
Cherry Creme Pie.. 188
Chocolate Raisin Pie 189
Choco-Vanilla Dream Pie....................................... 190
Coconut Creme Pie 191
Lemon Pineapple Pie... 191
Watergate Pie... 192
Cookie Crust 193
Frozen Pie Crust 193
Pie Crust 194
Graham Crumb Crust 194

COOKIES

Candy Bar Cookies 195, 196
Magic Cookie Bars... 196
German Pecan Slices 197

DESSERTS

Apple Crunch Bread Pudding.................................... 198
Banana Bread Pudding... 199
Brownies 199
Cherry Crunch Dessert... 200
Cinnamon Roll Breakfast Ring 200
Crunchy Pumpkin Squares 201
French Custard 202
French Toast 202
Hawaiian Pineapple Banana Creme Dessert or Pie 203
Pecan Filled Baked Pears....................................... 204
Sherried Fruit.. 204
Wine Gelatin Dessert.. 205

CANDY

Candy Hints 206
Chocolate Covered Strawberries 207
Chocolate Drops.. 208
Creamy Pralines 209
Heavenly Hash Candy.. 210
Million Dollar Fudge 211
Passion Pralines 212
Peanut Brittle 213
Pecan Crunch 214
2 Minute Fudge 214

PLEASE PRINT OR TYPE

NAME _____

ADDRESS _____

CITY _____ STATE _____ ZIP _____

Please send me _____ copies of Southern Spice at $11.95 each $ _____

Plus postage and handling costs of . . . . $1.50 each $ _____

Jefferson Parish residents must add 8% sales tax. All other Louisi-
ana residents must add 4% state tax . . . . each $ _____

Enclosed is my check ☐ or money order ☐ . . . . TOTAL $ _____

Please make checks payable to: **Pelican Publishing Company, Inc.**
Mailing Address: P.O. Box 189
Gretna, Louisiana 70054

PLEASE PRINT OR TYPE

NAME _____

ADDRESS _____

CITY _____ STATE _____ ZIP _____

Please send me _____ copies of Southern Spice at $11.95 each $ _____

Plus postage and handling costs of . . . . $1.50 each $ _____

Jefferson Parish residents must add 8% sales tax. All other Louisi-
ana residents must add 4% state tax . . . . each $ _____

Enclosed is my check ☐ or money order ☐ . . . . TOTAL $ _____

Please make checks payable to: **Pelican Publishing Company, Inc.**
Mailing Address: P.O. Box 189
Gretna, Louisiana 70054

PLEASE PRINT OR TYPE

NAME _____

ADDRESS _____

CITY _____ STATE _____ ZIP _____

Please send me _____ copies of Southern Spice at $11.95 each $ _____

Plus postage and handling costs of . . . . $1.50 each $ _____

Jefferson Parish residents must add 8% sales tax. All other Louisi-
ana residents must add 4% state tax . . . . each $ _____

Enclosed is my check ☐ or money order ☐ . . . . TOTAL $ _____

Please make checks payable to: **Pelican Publishing Company, Inc.**
Mailing Address: P.O. Box 189
Gretna, Louisiana 70054